SHIRLEY MITCHELL WILLIAMS

STAGE 4 CANCER GONE!

outskirtspress
DENVER, COLORADO

Stage 4 Cancer--Gone!

v2.0

http://www.facebook.com/shirleymitchellwilliams
www.shirleymwilliams.com

All Scriptural References were taken from the King James Version of the Bible.

Cover Image by Adam Holmes

Outskirts Press, Inc.
http://www.outskirtspress.com

ISBN: 978-1-4787-2540-4

PRINTED IN THE UNITED STATES OF AMERICA

Dedication

I would like to dedicate this book to all those daring to believe God for a miracle. Faith moves God! I pray this testimony of what Jesus did for me will reproduce thousands fold,

"...for the testimony of Jesus is the spirit of prophecy" (Revelation 19:10b).

Deep down, in the place where you say, "I know God", I pray the Holy Spirit will open the eyes of your understanding, and you will be ignited with a fire that will bring forth an engulfing inferno in your spirit that will explode and catapult you to go out and destroy the works of the enemy.

Go into all the world!

God's Word is true and forever!

Contents

Introduction

In this book, you will follow a time in my life from when I began to feel the pain of cancer` to being diagnosed with Stage 4 cancer, end stage, that had metastasized from my breast to my bones, down my vertebrae, to my ribs, into my pelvic and pubic areas, and even into some of my organs and lymph nodes. I pray that you will travel with me on my journey to being free of cancer – beginning with the time when I was given anywhere from three weeks to ninety days to live by some doctors until I came out on the other side – free of all cancer in every form!

As you read this account, you will see that I have left out nothing, including the fear, weakness, dread, and pain that I walked through side by side with the faith that was rising up inside of me. I am sure that there are those who have gone through cancer themselves who will readily recognize what they faced and felt because I have walked a similar path. I want you to see and experience the spiritual nature of my walk. I pray that what I heard, saw, felt, and received will not be lost to you, the reader. It was what I considered to be the key to all that came forth.

As you read this book, you may decide that the cancer was cured by the therapy, detox foot bath, sweating, vitamins, or a special diet. They were instruments in my deliverance from cancer; yet, they were not Christ, who is the true source of my healing. I believe this would be a grave error; instead, I wish to point you to the Lord Jesus Christ, who is the Word of God, to praying in the Holy Spirit, and to being led by the Spirit to go one way and not another. Your mind will be looking to define the cure, and when the story is over, you will agree with me that nutrition *does* play a big part in how we live, unlike one of the doctors who informed me that nutrition would not help me because the cancer had gone too far. I was surely not in agreement, and it was one of the directions I was led to take.

Still, I cannot stress enough that the need is to follow Christ Jesus and to hear His voice and stand on the Word of God. This journey if separated from the personal work of the Holy Spirit and His direction would leave us with a formula in the flesh without the power of God to bring everything to pass.

The promises I found in the Word of God are for all those who believe upon Jesus as their Lord -- no matter what they have done in the past, whether they have served God all of their life or just cried out to Jesus to save them today. All provision for all our needs, including healing, is available to whosoever will dare to believe God. Impossibilities bow to the name of Jesus. "With God, nothing shall be impossible to them that believe," Mark 9:23. As I immersed myself in the scriptures, my faith grew to new levels; and as I took one step at a time, I soon walked out of the pit of despair into life and life more abundantly. Sometimes, I felt as if I was soaking in the promises, and I would listen to the scriptures and know I was more than an overcomer through Christ Jesus; yet the next day, I would find myself struggling to even quote them against the pain and weakness that I was feeling. It was often as if every promise I would grasp one day would be shaken so severely the next that I had to continue to hear the Word to stand in faith. "But, when you have done all to stand, stand, take a hold of the truth, continue in the Word of God and the truth will set you free (Ephesians 6:13, John 8:32 compilation). I know and can now say with all my heart that all the promises of God in Christ are "Yes" and "Amen!" God is no respecter of persons; what He has done for me, He has made available for you! Only believe.

I pray that as you read this book of my journey, you will receive personal insight and reach out to take what has been made available through Jesus Christ Lord of all!

To all those who I encountered on the way to my recovery, many of whom have already passed on, I will never lose sight of this truth:

"For whether we live, we live unto the Lord; and whether we die, we die unto the Lord: whether we live therefore, or die, we are the Lord's" (Rom. 14:8).

Acknowledgements

I would like to thank my awesome, amazing husband, Mark, for never leaving my side and never wavering but standing in absolute faith in agreement with God. I love you forever!

I would like to thank my parents, Cordell W. and Odena L. Mitchell, for being such an incredible living example before me all of my life and showing me the heart of God. For that, I am eternally grateful.

Thank you to my brother, Mark, and his wife, Jenifer, who so willing gave it all to help us through a difficult time. We love you so much!

To our daughter, Shanee, who became my personal trainer and pushed me to get back into shape and never allowed me to give up -- Thank you for standing in faith with me.

To our daughter, Shatiel Amanda, and her husband, Adam, thank you for putting your life on hold to help me and blessing us with Amalee, our granddaughter, and Jaren, our grandson. Our lives are so enriched because of you.

To our son, Vaughn, who staggered not in unbelief but continued to stand and call upon God, reminding Him of His covenant and promises. Son, God's word is true; I am alive today because of what Jesus made available to every believer.

Thank you so much to my sister, Cindy, and her husband, Greg, for staying with the "stuff". "For who will hearken unto you in this matter? but as his part is that goeth down to the battle, so shall his part be that tarrieth by the stuff: they shall part alike" (I Samuel 30:24). Thank you for keeping the business running and taking care of so much at the church.

Thank you to our assistant pastors, Derek and Tonya Thurlby; our youth pastor, Tate Inderlied; our worship leaders, Daniel and Rebekah Whitehead; the *women's pastor, Betty Jones; and all those who kept the church and kept it all moving forward. Thank you all for your years of service.*

Thank you to my cousins, Keith and Stephanie Sepulveda and Tiffany Dilts, for all your direction in the food department and your deep compassion to help me and my family.

Thank you to my Uncle Farris and Aunt Susan Whitehead, who rose up in faith and went before us to show us the way.

Thank you to my father-in-law and mother-in-law, French B. & Patricia A. Williams, for all your help. You took care of so much to help us through this time, and I am so grateful for you both.

Thank you to Celeste Canedo, Elisha Holmes, Tonya Thurlby for helping me push the book through to completion.

Thank you to all those who faithfully supported us while we ran through the Valley of the Shadow of Death.

Preface

This is a story about the remarkable journey of a woman's faith. When she was diagnosed with Stage IV, end-stage breast cancer, she decided that she would fight this with all means necessary to get well. Through her faith in God and with what medical science has to offer, along with conventional and non-conventional therapy, her health has been restored. This is an inspiring book that I recommend for those with and those without cancer. This will truly touch your heart.

Jairo Olivares, MD-Texas Oncology

Specializing in Medical Oncology and Hematology

~I was lead to Dr. Olivares by the Holy Spirit and he was instrumental in opening the eyes of my understanding in the areas of health and nutrition that have changed my life forever.~

The Diagnosis

"Stage 4 Cancer!" I was stunned. *How could this be?* The doctor's words echoed inside of me; she told me that the cancer had metastasized in my bones, organs and lymph nodes, and I only had about ninety days to live. *There is no way!* My mind and emotions began to whirl around as fear, dizziness, and weakness tried to overtake me. I was in a state of shock! My physical body began to tremble and pain started increasing all over my body as fear tried to overtake me. How could this happen? Surely, this was a mistake! I have never even smoked. I have always tried to be good to people and obey my parents. I prayed often. In my mind, I cried out, "God, I have served you all my life. This can't be right!" My mind continued to race. I had rigorously followed all that I knew to do to stay healthy, and I did not understand how this could happen to me! At the young age of forty-five with one daughter married, one daughter in college, and a son of fourteen, now, according to the doctors, I was facing death and quickly.

My Father and Mother

All of us, in a large part, are products of what was poured into us growing up, and I was no different:

Behold, every one that useth proverbs shall use this proverb against thee, saying, As is the mother, so is her daughter (Ezekiel 16:44).

My father and mother seemed to be constantly in prayer, reading the Bible, or fasting. These three things made up the life that I personally witnessed in my parents. It was so normal to see praying and fasting taking place for days or weeks that I actually thought everyone else did it as well.

Early rising to pray was normal, not just on special occasions but every day. I learned the serious nature of the things of God by watching how my parents took everything that was related to the Scriptures or church. It seemed as though it was the most important thing in their lives.

Now, understand, my parents were pastors of churches my entire childhood, and being in church and Sunday school – plus Sunday night and midweek services – would be considered sufficient by most parents but not mine.

Our parent's devotion to our spiritual upbringing was astounding. We would have personal Bible time seven nights a week even if we had just come from church. In those seven years, there is something I received that I cannot put my finger on that affected my outlook on life. I could see that the things of God were valuable to my mother and father, and now, they were important to me as well. I could see it in them, and it was in me.

Salvation, conversion, a born-again experience, baptism in the Holy Ghost, praying in the Holy Ghost, water baptism, communion, and a call to preach the word of God were things that came separately; yet, it was all part of life in Christ. These became a ball of fire in my life as I was surrounded and carried deeper and deeper into the knowledge of the Lord and Savior for whom my soul longed. I desired to know him as Paul:

That I may know him, and the power of his resurrection, and the fellowship of his sufferings, being made conformable unto his death; (Philippians 3:10)

Over the years, I had become more keenly aware of the sufferings of Jesus on the cross. This was not a moment or an event, rather a growing sense of His sacrifice on the cross. The sermons my father preached were graphic and intense, especially when it came to the cross. All of this awareness became mine as well. When I was in elementary school, I would preach from the top of the monkey bars on the playground and many would come to know Jesus as Lord. I would try to imitate my daddy; little did I realize that the one who was in my father was in me also.

I am crucified with Christ: nevertheless I live; yet not I, but Christ liveth in me: and the life which I now live in the flesh I live by the faith of the Son of God, who loved me, and gave himself for me. (Galatians 2:20)

Like her mother, my mother was a quiet woman. She had been in a family of eight children who were raised on a farm as sharecroppers working their own farm, as well as her daddy hiring out all the family to work other farms. When they got in from school, they went straight to the field. On Saturdays, or days when there was no school, they stayed all day in the field. Sundays were such a relief: those were church days, and everyone got dressed up to go to Sunday School and church – how wonderful, no work in the field, a day of rest!

My mother was quiet but not silent. The children heard her in a thousand ways as we picked up on who she was, her serious nature toward the things of God, her love for her husband, and the desire for her children to serve God.

Her mother, my grandmother, also had a quiet spirit about her; arguing and fighting was not in the home. If anyone raised his voice, it would be Grandpa, not Grandma. She had come from a large family of farmers with thirteen children. Grandma's family had been swept into the kingdom of God early through the Pentecostal revival that had swept through the country at that time. They, too, had been set afire with the things of God.

My great-grandmother had raised a family of thirteen children and all but two stayed with their spouses all their lives. My grandmother had raised a family of eight of which six had avoided divorce; and now, I had come from a family of four children, and after thirty years, all still are married to their spouses.

Now, here I was, forty-five and having come from three generations of quiet but strong women who had carried their own weight and then some. Now, I just felt weakness all over my body. I leaned on my husband. I was facing death with only a few days left. I didn't feel as strong as I once had. My husband quoted the promises of God both to me and over me.

My parents were also deep in prayer and a source of strength. My daddy was waiting on God. He was certain we would receive the direction we needed from the Spirit of God and the Word of God.

My sheep hear my voice, and I know them, and they follow me (John 10:27).

If I ever needed to hear from heaven, it was now.

I Questioned the Pain.

One day in 2011, I was at the flooring and furniture store we own, and a customer needed a roll of carpet. I squatted down to lift it with my shoulder as I have for many years, but when I tried to lift the roll of carpet, it was wedged up against another roll of carpet. So, while lifting with my legs and the roll on my shoulder, I grabbed the end of the roll with my right hand and pushed with my right arm. When I did, I felt something snap in the right side of my chest, and I felt like I was hemorrhaging inside. I felt so much pain that I immediately stopped and laid my hand on my chest and began to command my body to be whole in the name of Jesus. The pain subsided after a while. Over the next couple of months, I took it very easy and tried to not lift anything heavy with my right arm.

Around six months later, we had a load of heavy sofas arrive, and they were unloaded on our parking lot. It looked as if it was going to rain, so my cousin, Derek, and I went to quickly move a Flexsteel brand sofa, which is very heavy, and we carried it into the store. When I did, I felt I had re-injured my chest. I stopped and prayed again. It seemed to be okay, but from that point, things began to change.

I kept praying for myself but not as I had always done. I had been very tired for about a year or more and found myself not praying as much or spending enough time in the word. I was busy trying to keep up with just the necessities but felt like I couldn't get enough rest. I would fall asleep easily. I had felt like I needed to go see a doctor, but I also felt like I would be doubting and unbelieving if I did. I continued to pray in the Holy Spirit and continued to feel the Holy Spirit leading me in that direction. For years, I had felt like I needed to get busy exercising and eating right. We were doing fine financially, so we would eat out more than we should just for convenience. The pain in my chest, especially my right side, had gotten worse; however, the thing that made me think that I needed to do something beyond prayer was when I noticed a large knot about the size of a child's fist that seemed to materialize in my breast, seemingly almost overnight -- then my nipple inverted. I kept thinking it was all a result of a torn muscle but little did I know what was going on in other areas of my body!

I began noticing that I couldn't remember things, too. I had always been very sharp and quick mentally. I had graduated valedictorian of my high school and now found myself not being able to remember names and telephone numbers. One day, I left my office and went to my vehicle, but when I began to punch in the code on my vehicle, I couldn't remember it. I had locked my purse and keys in my vehicle. Everyone else had left the office, and someone else locked up behind me because I had left my keys to the office in my purse. I stopped and began to cry out to God, "What is going on with me? God, I don't understand. Help me Lord!" Right after that, I remembered the key code and got in and drove myself home.

I had studied accounting and received my Enrolled Agent license through the Internal Revenue Service, so I was accustomed to recalling telephone numbers for clients and their Social Security numbers as well. But now, I found myself struggling to even think right. It was as if I was in a mental fog that I couldn't shake off.

About five years earlier, Mark and I went on a trip to Africa to minister in Kenya and Uganda with another minister from Oklahoma, Mark McIntosh. Before our visas were issued from Africa, we needed to obtain a copy of my shot record. I went to my local physician's office where I had received my hepatitis vaccine years prior when I worked as a medic for the Brewster County Ambulance Service – local protocol required a hepatitis vaccination. A few years later, I became the Justice of the Peace and along with that came the position of the county coroner; so, offices required another round of hepatitis vaccinations. My records were not readily available from the physician's office, and the assistant at his office suggested that I should probably just take yet another round of hepatitis vaccinations to ensure that I was fully inoculated before heading to Africa. I felt uneasy about more vaccines, but the nurse encouraged me that it was better to be safe than sorry. It took several months for the full vaccine to be administered. Even after the hepatitis shots began, I had to drive to a larger city just to get my yellow fever vaccination, which was necessary to acquire the visas for the trip. I really felt led to go to Africa and know that we must be led by the Spirit of God and never allow fear to lead us in any way. So, we went, and God did wondrously on this trip.

My left hip began to bother me a few years before we went to Africa, and I had gone to a chiropractor and gotten an adjustment and seemed to be better, but off and on, it would hurt me. I started exercising, thinking my back was out of alignment and was sure that was what had been causing my hip to hurt. I noticed that the more I swam the better I felt, but the weather turned cooler, and the water was too cold to swim in; so, I stopped exercising altogether.

Also around this time, I had felt a very small knot in my right breast, and I went into prayer and fasting and felt led to fast all sugar, breads and packaged foods, and it went away. After a period of time, I went to the doctor just for a checkup, and he told me it was nothing to worry about.

My left hip continued to hurt, and I was having a hard time sleeping. I was becoming lethargic, and things were just not processing correctly in my brain. Many times, I was thinking one thing, and I would say something else. I had never experienced anything like this. I kept blaming it on a lack of sleep due to a mattress that was too hard; so, my husband began to tackle the chore of trying to make me comfortable and decided to change out our mattress (It's a good thing that we sell mattresses.). I would think the mattress was too hard, and my husband just kept changing it out. This actually became a joke: Shirley was like the princess and the pea. It was so hilarious the last couple of times we changed out the mattress because my husband and the boys would take the mattress and throw it over our upstairs balcony, so he didn't have to carry it down the stairs. But, I wasn't about to laugh where he could see me because I knew it was quite difficult, and besides, I had really been hurting and wanted relief. One time, he even changed the mattress while I was gone, and our daughter, Shanee, made up the bed just the way I always did. No one said a word to me until morning, trying to surprise me and see if I noticed. I still didn't sleep well.

I made trip after trip to the chiropractor, and he would frequent our place of business and adjust me. I stood on my head at times, trying to get some relief, and even got onto an inversion table thinking that would help. Nothing helped.

I Decided to Go to the Doctor.

I had always stood on God's word, and this time was no different. One night, I had a hard time sleeping. My underarm was now beginning to hurt more and more, and the pain in my right breast and chest area had grown progressively worse. The knot inside my breast had grown to about the size of a child's fist. A few days later, my nipple inverted; this did not look good!

As we drove to Midland, Texas, the next morning, I told Mark that I felt I needed to see a doctor. Mark's response was, "Well, since that is the last thing I would have ever expected you to say, you should call the doctor and see if he can get you in."

Picking up my cell phone, I called a doctor in Odessa. I explained to him that I thought I had torn a muscle in my chest. The receptionist informed me that they happened to have a cancellation, and they would be able to see me; so, we drove straight to the doctor's office. Going to the doctor was unusual for me, as I have always depended on God to be my healer. If I or any of my family members became ill, I prayed; we prayed; – and stood on God's word for healing.

By the time we arrived at the medical office, my nerves were more than just a little shaken, and deep in my spirit, I knew that today would mark a permanent change in my life.

During our meeting with the doctor, Mark received a phone call about a job he was working on and stepped out of the room in the middle of the examination. It was during my husband's brief absence that the doctor looked at me and stated, "I don't think you have a torn muscle; I think you have breast cancer." I could not believe what I was hearing! My doctor went on to tell me he wanted me to go get a mammogram and an ultrasound as soon as possible; he picked up his cell phone and called the hospital.

Upon leaving the doctor's office, Mark and I drove to the hospital which was just a few blocks away. After waiting for what seemed to be two hours, my doctor surprised us at the hospital. He had come to check up on me. Frustrated that I had not been seen yet, he said, "Follow me. I have a friend who is a doctor that can get you in for a CAT scan, today."

The doctor told me he was very concerned about me. Mark and I drove to the second location – the clinic my doctor recommended – only to find ourselves waiting for another couple of hours until we ultimately were told that I could not be seen that day.

Mark and I left that hospital, ran our errands and drove home. I was sick in my stomach the rest of that day. In a state of shock, I remember not knowing what to think or do. My mind was restless as I began to examine every part of myself: my spirit, my heart, and all that it harbored. I began to question if I had any unforgiveness toward anyone. Deeply troubled, I began to repent for anything and everything I could think of. I still had not come to terms with my doctor's diagnosis, and I could not bring myself to tell Mark what the doctor said when Mark had left the room.

Mark and I drove home: a two and a half hour drive, but it seemed like the drive was especially long that day. My physical pain seemed to intensify by merely thinking about the words the doctor had spoken. My mind was racing. I questioned how it was possible that cancer could have ever touched my body when I had served God all of my life. I suppose, deep down inside, I really hoped and tried to convince myself that the doctor was mistaken. I justified my denial by telling myself, "He wasn't a cancer doctor."

The same day, my husband was reading his Bible when he felt like the Holy Spirit was speaking to him about a certain verse:

And Abraham said unto his young men, Abide ye here with the ass; and I and the lad will go yonder and worship, and come again to you. (Genesis 22:5)

(A Rhema word is a word that is spoken directly to you from the Lord. My father received a word the same day that he felt was a Rhema word, also:

When Jesus heard that, he said, This sickness is not unto death, but for the glory of God, that the Son of God might be glorified thereby. (John 11:4))

At that moment, I remembered a night several years ago when I received a phone call from a man in our church while I was at the grocery store. He and his wife were at the hospital, and his wife had just delivered a baby boy;the man was crying and screaming. I tried to get him to calm down and tell me what was wrong. He kept crying, "God help us!" I left the grocery store and went straight to the hospital. When I walked into the room where the family was, I heard a scripture. *'Who was it that sinned that the child was born this way, was it the father or the mother?"*

And his disciples asked him, saying, Master, who did sin, this man, or his parents, that he was born blind? 3. Jesus answered, Neither hath this man sinned, nor his parents: but that the works of God should be made manifest in him (John 9:2-3).

I walked into the room to see the father on his knees, crying. I looked at the baby boy and noticed that he was born with a birth defect, missing a couple of toes, part of his foot, and one leg much shorter and thinner than the other. I knew that with God nothing would be impossible. Over the next two years, we saw many miracles in the boy's life as we pressed in to see the works of God being manifested. We saw the boy's foot grow out in front of the entire church one Sunday morning as I held the boy and felt his leg grow out. God gave the boy a missing ankle bone and hip bone. The doctors had said the boy would never crawl or walk because he was missing the proper bones and joints; but we saw that, with God, nothing would be impossible. Through several words of knowledge, standing on God's word, and never giving up on the promises of God, the boy now runs and plays. All the promises of God are "yea" and "amen" to me:

For all the promises of God in him are yea, and in him Amen, unto the glory of God by us. (II Corinthians 1:20)

My Doctor Called Me: "This Is Serious!"

Then saith he to Thomas, Reach hither thy finger, and behold my hands; and reach hither thy hand, and thrust it into my side: and be not faithless, but believing. (John 20:27)

~My father called me today with this scripture; it had come into my his heart, and it would not go away. He had called to tell us about it. A waging war was going on in my mind. ~

It was April 2012, and I was at the furniture store on a Saturday morning when my doctor called me. A week had passed since my initial visit with him. He asked me how I was doing and when the appointment was scheduled to get my scan. I told him I had rescheduled for the following week. He asked that I let him know as soon as it was done. Before ending our conversation, he said, "Please don't hide your head in the sand; this is serious."

This was a very difficult time for me. I had always believed God and knew that it was God's will to heal, but I was having a hard time with all of this: The internal struggle of knowing God's will and dealing with the thoughts and fears that were trying to dictate to me what I would and would not do, the physical pain that wouldn't go away, and the tumors that were multiplying. I knew the Word of God was true, but now the Holy Spirit would lead me down a path of new revelation that would begin with the authority that had been given to me when I called upon Jesus.

CAT Scan Results

My sister, Cindy, had a dream one morning in which she was telling me angrily not to cancel the appointment with the doctor.

I had another scripture that dropped into my heart after I put off going back to the doctor. He called me and insisted that I come in and get the tests done. This scripture was just inside me from out of nowhere; it was like it was alive:

And he said unto them, Why are ye so fearful? how is it that ye have no faith? (Mark 4:40)

Three weeks after seeing the doctor about my pain and the large knot, I went in for a CAT scan to another doctor. As it usually goes with these things, I could not get my results until the doctor who read the CAT scans contacted the doctor who ordered the scan in the first place, and the two discussed the findings. So, I continued to wait; even though it was just overnight, it seemed like forever.

It was a hot, windy, West Texas day, and Mark and I were in Odessa checking on our church bus that was in the shop getting some repairs when I finally received a call from my doctor. Mark was with the shop personnel, and I was standing outside of the shop when the call came in. I walked across the parking lot to my vehicle and got in, so I could hear more clearly since the wind was blowing so hard. He told me the mass in my breast indeed looked like cancer, and I would need to get myself to MD Anderson Cancer Center in Houston, Texas, or my nearest Texas Oncology Center to see a breast surgeon who deals with cancer patients. As the doctor was speaking these words, I was immensely troubled and trying with all my strength to hold myself together emotionally. The fear attempting to grip me was so strong I began to immediately speak God's word over my mind, my will, and my emotions. After what seemed like hours had gone by (even though it wasn't but just about thirty minutes), Mark came to the vehicle; he could tell that I was shook up. I finally brought myself to tell my husband about the phone call as well as what the doctor had stated during the first visit. I could tell Mark was very concerned, and he chose his words very carefully. I remember one of the first things he said was, "There is not a weapon that has been formed against us that will prosper." I then called my mother and father, our eldest daughter, and my sister.

After I told my sister, Cindy, what the doctor said, she began doing some research of her own on the internet. Cindy found a doctor at Texas Oncology in the Dallas, Texas, area. I called, and an appointment was set for May 15th.

Mark and I were very optimistic as we drove to my appointment. We had been praying and fasting over this whole situation, and we truly believed everything was going to be all right. Mark shared a dream with me: he said he dreamed that when we went to see the doctor I was told the tumor was benign. We took this as further confirmation that everything was going to be fine. We thought to ourselves, "Surely, there will be no cancer."

Bid Me to Come on the Water

~We stopped by to see my father and mother in Midland, Texas, as we headed out to Dallas. My father gave me a scripture that he believed was a word specifically for me.

And Peter answered him and said, Lord, if it be thou, bid me come unto thee on the water (Matthew 14:28).

My father told me that I would be faced with a decision as to which way to go; the Holy Spirit would show me which way was His way, and I was to take it.~

These words would soon prove to be accurate.

It is the spirit that quickeneth; the flesh profiteth nothing: the words that I speak unto you, they are spirit, and they are life (John 6:63).

The Ultrasound Showed Tumors.

For she said, If I may touch but his clothes, I shall be whole (Mark 5:28).

When my parents were serving as missionaries overseas, my dad had received this scripture for a Samoan woman in a hospital in Western Samoa. He had prayed for seven days, reading this portion of scripture to her and having her read it each day over and over. On the seventh day, she relayed that she saw Jesus pass by her, and she reached out and touched his clothes. The blood and water draining from her lungs stopped, and she was healed.

We traveled to McKinney, Texas, on May 14, 2012. We arrived at Texas Oncology on the morning of May 15, 2012, to see another doctor for an ultrasound, a mammogram, and a biopsy. The room was full of gowned women whose faces showed they were in terror; you could see by the look on their faces that they were being tormented with thoughts. I had more tests to be done. The ultrasound showed tumors all over my breast in all four quadrants.

I was reminded of this Scripture deep inside my spirit that very evening:

But now thus saith the LORD that created thee, O Jacob, and he that formed thee, O Israel, Fear not: for I have redeemed thee, I have called thee by thy name; thou art mine. 2. When thou passest through the waters, I will be with thee; and through the rivers, they shall not overflow thee: when thou walkest through the fire, thou shalt not be burned; neither shall the flame kindle upon thee (Isaiah 43:1-2).

Lighten the Ship.

And when they had eaten enough, they lightened the ship, and cast out the wheat into the sea (Acts 27:38).

Early that morning, May 14, 2012, my dad was up praying (thank God for praying parents!) and had a vision of the Apostle Paul on board a ship and the men (fellow sailors) were throwing everything off the ship to lighten the ship. He instructed us to let everything go around us and delegate authority to others in the church, so we could be released from the care of the church and our store. Then, we could be free of stress and be able to just concentrate on hearing God and following Him. My husband and I decided to do just that. I didn't realize just how attached I was to so many things, so it was a challenge to shake loose of so much. For years, it was so much easier for me to just do certain things instead of training someone else to do it, and many times having to go back and redo it myself, but I see now that I was wrong. I never wanted people to feel overwhelmed or overworked at that church, so I did so much myself. I was the one that was overwhelmed and overworked. There were times I was so tired and wouldn't dare leave until everything was done. I felt like people wouldn't come to church and hear the word of God if there was work to be done. I did so much out of duty. I was committed to a fault, involved in so many areas, many of which were self induced, and had a severe case of a false sense of responsibility; but soon, we did it. We broke loose-- throwing over one thing, then another, and another until the ship was lightened. When I walked away from so much, I came back to see that many people were helping in many areas, and I asked my sister where the help came from. She said that they were there all the time. I just wouldn't get out of the way. That was a shock; now, the people were owning something and taking care of it, and I didn't know how to respond. I cried and repented, knowing that God had truly sent help, and He was taking a load off of me.

The Biopsy

Upon our arrival to the doctor's office, I was handed several forms that needed to be completed. Not paying attention too much to those around me, I sat down and began to fill out the paperwork. It was not until I took a moment to look around that I saw the dreary condition of the women accompanying me in the waiting area. Many had no hair or hair that was just beginning to grow back. Several of the women were very skinny, and some appeared to be very sick – I assumed from chemotherapy. Others sat somberly in wheelchairs, unable to walk from weakness. The grim scene reminded me of a concentration camp. The air of despondency weighing down on the women in the waiting room was disheartening. Time seemed to pass by lethargically, and my wait to be seen seemed like an eternity. I exhaled deeply when I finally heard them call, "Shirley Williams." I got up and followed the nurse into a room where I waited to see the doctor.

A doctor walked in. I started our visit by telling her about how I believed I had injured myself when I had picked up a heavy roll of carpet at our furniture store and how I was sure the lump and pain in my chest area was nothing more than a torn muscle. She calmly responded, "Well, let's take a look." As she began to examine my breast, she paused, looked at me, and said, "You have breast cancer."

I was so disturbed; it was very difficult trying to swallow. My grandmother had recently died, and we found out she had breast cancer. My grandmother's sister had also died of breast cancer when she was in her forties. All the thoughts suddenly racing in my head were hard to commandeer. I was crying out on the inside but still trying to contain my emotions and composure. I had always been so strong, and ready to be there for everyone else, but now, it was me, needing help.

She proceeded to tell me that she wanted me to have a biopsy performed, right away. I had developed some markings that looked like terrible stretch marks that ran down the sides of my breast, and it wasn't until later that I found out that those were yet another sign of breast cancer. The doctor began making phone calls to get approval from my insurance company, and it wasn't long before I was sitting in a room filled with women, all of whom were wearing thin, pale-colored hospital gowns and all waiting on a doctor or a procedure to be performed. Like me, some women were waiting for mammograms but not all. I could see that some had already gone through surgery and had one or both breasts removed. Several women were crying uncontrollably, while the rest of the women had sunk in their chairs like zombies. Their countenances seemed vacant of all emotions. It seemed as if their hearts and bodies had been completely drained, and all that was left was an echoing emptiness behind their glossed-over eyes. No one was speaking to anyone; it was distressing to see what these women were going through.

After my mammogram, I was taken into the next room for an ultrasound. During the ultrasound, I noticed the technician marking several places with a cursor on the image of my right breast depicted on the screen. Although each time I would ask a question, I was told I would have to wait until I spoke to my doctor. The technician's refusal to explain what he was marking and measuring on the screen concerned me. I thought, "Why is he being so secretive?" As he continued clicking and measuring and clicking and measuring, it reminded me of the ultrasounds I experienced when I was pregnant. Only this time, instead of clicking and measuring a baby's head, he was doing it to my breast, repeatedly. I asked myself, "Surely, all those can't be tumors; can they?"

I was moved back to the other side of the building near the examination room where I had initially been placed, and I was prepped for a needle biopsy. The doctor had a machine that she placed on my breast over the areas where they had found tumors. Then the doctor using this machine proceeded to take plugs out of my breast by inserting a long, cylindrical instrument – about the diameter of a standard pencil – into my flesh. The instrument was hollow in the center, like a straw with a razor-sharp end that literally would slice into the breast as it was being inserted. The machine would make a noise, suction, and extract a plug of my breast. I was shocked. This was definitely no skinny needle! The doctor had given me a shot of Lidocaine, a local anesthetic, to numb the area, but it did not work on me. I felt everything! I started shaking, as tears ran down my face. The doctor asked, "Can you feel that?" I said, "Yes!" She gave me another shot and another; yet, I continued to writhe in pain. My legs shook intensely, and I began praying in the Holy Spirit, crying out loud, "Jesus! Jesus!" The doctor said, "You cannot feel that." I screamed, "Yes, I can!" She asked me what I felt, and I told her I could feel her sticking something into my breast and a suction machine was sucking out part of my breast. I told her I could feel the blood running down my breast into my armpit and onto my neck. The doctor replied, "There is no way." She turned to the nurse and said, "Get me another shot! Stat!" After the procedure was complete, and I was calming down, the doctor told me that she had been performing biopsies for years, and she had never given anyone that much pain killer and was shocked I did not respond to it. I later discovered that my mother did not respond to Lidocaine, either.

I Heard a Still, Small Voice in the MRI.

I was soon waiting for my next procedure, the MRI. Mark had been patiently waiting outside in the hallway in the waiting area, praying the entire time. While the nurse who was prepping me proceeded to inject me with a contrast solution for the procedure, she began talking to me. She said, "Something is so wrong." I asked what she meant, and she replied, "Years ago, all we ever saw here were women over fifty with breast cancer, but now, we are seeing twelve-year-old girls and boys with breast cancer. It must be our food!" I continued to listen to her as I lay waiting on a gurney for what was next.

She explained how that she was concerned about all the GMO (genetically modified organisms), the food that we eat today is not like it was years ago. The United States of America had allowed GMOs to come into the county and we don't even realize how much our food has been altered, our bodies are receiving so many toxins and it is hard for the body to elimate all the poison. All the pesticides on our fruits and vegetables is so dangerous, strawberries are some of the worst. Our chicken is packed with estrogen to get the chicken breast to grow, then we consume it and little boys begin to develop breast and the little girls develop much earlier than they should, this is all so wrong. The GMOs have greatly effected the corn crops, and around 97% of all of our food has some form of corn or a by product of corn. Look at all the packages, corn syrup is in so many products. We must all be aware of what we are putting into our bodies and feeding our children.

Another attendant arrived and I was wheeled into a room with a large machine. I had to climb up on a small ladder to get into this one. I was instructed to lie on my stomach with my arms up and my breasts hanging down. My heart was racing at this point. Those thoughts I had succeeded in controlling thus far were literally starting a battle in my mind.

As I crawled into the machine, I heard a still, small voice say to me, "I am coming to heal you." Those words resounded through me and filled me with a great sense of peace, even though I was still bleeding from the biopsy and in so much pain. That day proved to be a very difficult day! I simply wanted to go home and rest; instead, we went to a hotel and stayed there that night – home was a nine-hour drive away.

I returned to the doctor's office to receive the biopsy results, two days later. She told me that the biopsy had confirmed I had cancer. She told me I was to start chemotherapy and radiation treatment right away, and that surgery was inevitable: a mastectomy.

"We have to get the tumors to shrink first," she said. "The tumors are in all four quadrants of your breast, and there is no way to save any of it." She said she was concerned because the MRI showed that the cancer had metastasized into some of my bones, including my sternum, clavicle, and ribs. I asked her about nutritional options, and she told me that nutrition definitely would not be the answer, and it would not help. She said, "Don't you turn away from chemo and radiation, the traditional treatments. These are your only hope." I was greatly troubled by those words because I knew that God was my hope, and through Him, nothing was impossible.

The doctor went on to inform me that she wanted me to get a PET (positron emission tomography) scan immediately and would try to get me in right away. (PET uses nuclear medicine to produce three-dimensional images of body functions.) The doctor was clearly upset and was pushing me to begin treatment without delay. I was unsettled inside and knew there had to be other options. The Bible says that we will go out with joy and be led forth with peace, and I definitely did not have peace. I wanted another opinion.

My unwillingness to settle with the first oncologist's diagnosis and plan of action did not stem from my lack of trust in her wanting to do the right thing but from my own reservations I had developed by working closely with many doctors in the past. I had worked as an emergency medical technician for about eighteen years, in hospice for several years, and had served as county coroner for ten years. I had worked around many doctors and had observed them in practice long enough to learn that they all did the best they could, within the perimeters of their training. Having witnessed the struggles that many doctors faced with difficult situations beyond their scope of training, and realizing they were only human and there was a limit to the knowledge they possessed, when given my diagnosis, I knew I needed to be diligent in my search for alternative options.

I found it difficult to believe how much pressure many doctors tried to put on me. Believing they all must have meant well, I could not help but empathize with what Elijah must have felt when he experienced the wind, the earthquake, and the fire. God was not in any of those things. He was in the still, small voice. That was the voice I needed to hear from heaven.

And he said, Go forth, and stand upon the mount before the LORD. And, behold, the LORD passed by, and a great and strong wind rent the mountains, and brake in pieces the rocks before the LORD; but the LORD was not in the wind: and after the wind an earthquake; but the LORD was not in the earthquake: 12. And after the earthquake a fire; but the LORD was not in the fire: and after the fire a still small voice (I Kings 19:11-12).

God was in the still, small voice. Jesus would repeat this verse in the New Testament in different words:

My sheep hear my voice, and I know them, and they follow me: (John 10:27)

Speaking the Word of God over My Body

We went back to Texas Oncology. The doctor told me that I had Stage 4 Cancer, and because the cancer had spread into my bones, the doctor said that she had scheduled a full-body PET scan the following morning at 5:45 to detect the cancer in any other areas of my body. She said the PET scan would reveal any further spread of cancer into my soft tissues or organs.

The doctor said that this was very important and not to delay in seeking chemotherapy and surgery. Then she reiterated that this was nothing to wait on. The doctor became very stern when I told her we would go home and pray about it.

We went to a hotel nearby to rest. We called our kids back home, five hundred and fifty miles away, to tell them why we were staying another day. After such news, it was hard to keep from sounding alarmed.

We then went to the Baylor Hospital in Plano, Texas, for a full-body PET scan. I remember going to the hospital early that morning and believing that whatever had been in my body would be gone by the time I had the scan. We agreed that the righteous are bold as a lion coming into agreement with God concerning His salvation for our spirit, soul, and body.

I had always prayed for the sick, and I had seen so many healed and so many delivered from seemingly hopeless situations that I knew God was not a respecter of persons, so I believed with all my heart that healing was provided through the work of the cross for me. I had been speaking the Word of God over my body and would continue.

My First Ray of Hope

And there appeared unto them Elias with Moses: and they were talking with Jesus (Mark 9:4).

~I was thinking about this scripture today but I really could not attach a meaning, so we just went on and kept it in our mind, pondering, "What does this mean?"~

We were in McKinney for an MRI. Afterward, we would meet with my Uncle Farris and Aunt Susan Whitehead at the Healing Arts Cancer & Wellness Center in Richardson, Texas, and I would later understand that there was an application of Moses and Elijah to my situation. Both of these Bible figures had gone through what Jesus was about to go through: death itself or passing over the line between this world in the flesh and the next. The Moses and Elijah references had been pointing me to the events of that day when we would talk with Farris and Susan. They had already been through what I was facing. What a day! I knew there was life after a cancer diagnosis!

My Uncle Farris was diagnosed with multiple myeloma bone cancer some eight years prior and had suffered through many years of different processes, methods, radiation, and drugs before going to Dr. June (board certified in integrative medicine), who focused Uncle Farris' attention toward building his blood and immune systems through diet and nutritional supplements. My Uncle Farris' testimony of how the Lord had carried him was a breath of fresh air. He was living and breathing before us today. He endured many experimental drugs and homeopathic medicine while on this road; my uncle had been very sick and in a lot of pain and had almost died several times. After a period of time, his daughter found a nutritionist, and the family took him there. He had been given less than two weeks to live at that time, and his bodily functions had already shut down thirty percent when he entered the clinic. He began to receive nutritional IVs and fresh vegetable juices and took many supplements: a small bowl full at every meal. We had all been praying for his recovery and believing for a miracle. Within two weeks of being at this cancer wellness center, he began to gain strength. He continued to stay there for months and got stronger and stronger. He and his wife learned so much about eating organic foods and how important nutrition really is. The main purpose was to keep all the healthy cells healthy so there was no further breakdown in the body – no matter what type of treatment you were taking. There is so much that we all need to learn ***and apply*** to our lives to get healthy and stay healthy. We serve the God that heals and keeps us well, but we all need to learn how to listen and obey.

Dr. June, the nutritionist, had stressed that nutrition should promote a patient's immune system to help the body fight against diseases like cancer. She went over a diet with me, and it consisted of taking all sugar out of my diet, including removing all fruit, honey, and agave nectar – it made no difference whether it was natural or artificial (It is so precious to see how the Holy Spirit had been leading me for years in this direction, and now, there was a doctor reiterating it). If it was sweet, it was out. I found out that cancer loves sugar, and cancer feeds on sugar. Also, all dairy products were taken out of my diet. Only organic foods and whole grains were allowed, true whole foods. I could have two tablespoons of butter and two tablespoons of extra virgin olive oil everyday, but that was the only fat I could intake. I could have all the vegetables I wanted but was limited to no more than twelve ounces of organic meat a day. No pork was allowed at all (I understand it is more difficult for the body to digest), and nothing processed, mainly because of all the nitrates and nitrites. I was unaware of just how much processing was taking place in our foods. I began to find out about genetically modified organisms and found it to be disturbing.

I made a decision to eat to live instead of living to eat. The nutritionist recommended that I begin juicing immediately: four carrots, one small beet, and one medium cucumber every day and then add wheat grass juice. I began immediately implementing everything I learned and have continued to be very strict with my diet. I began to experiment with all types of recipes., and also found that I could have organic yogurt and kefir (a quarter of a cup each per day). I have always enjoyed cooking, which is a good thing since everything I could now eat had to be prepared from scratch.

Later, we drove from the clinic to Cleburne to stay with my Uncle Farris and Aunt Susan for the night, and so we stopped by Eastern Heights Church, where Uncle Farris pastored. He saw that I was very shaken up and encouraged me as he had always done and prayed with Mark and I. We then drove down the road a short distance to visit with our dear friends and missionaries, Rory and Flora Smithee. We shared with them what I was facing, and Rory rose up and declared, "We will run through this." We knew he was prophesying over us, and we grabbed ahold of those words by faith. Flora is a very small, native Mayan Indian, but there is nothing small about her in the spirit; she is a mighty warrior of God Almighty. She prayed explosively by the spirit. I needed faith surrounding me and guarded myself against any doubt and unbelief, which was very difficult. There are so many well-meaning Christians who are so full of doubt and unbelief, I had to begin to set up boundaries to protect myself.

My Fourth Opinion

After meeting with the nutritionist, I was told about another doctor who was a breast surgeon with Texas Oncology. I called to make an appointment. My meeting with her proved to be very trying. This doctor was very forceful and direct. She told me that she disagreed with the other doctor. Instead, she recommended that I schedule and undergo surgery immediately then begin chemotherapy and radiation treatment after the surgery was complete.

She performed a physical examination on me, and it really hurt! I was already swollen and in so much pain from all the other examinations and procedures that I had endured. My breast was bruised black and blue and covered with bandages from the multiple biopsies the previous doctor had taken from me; yet, none of these were as painful as I knew surgery would be.

The doctor told me that she would simply remove my breasts and make me a pair of new ones, and my insurance would cover it. This doctor seemed to be trying to encourage me. She went on to tell me that the cancer had advanced too far to save my nipple; but, not to worry, she would make new ones (she just failed to tell me the nipples would be tattooed). I know I was probably just another number and patient she had seen; yet, I wanted to hear compassion and empathy, especially when dealing with body parts being removed, loss of hair, etc..

I was dismayed and hungered for compassion, but instead, I found doctors who had become hardened by their day-to-day dealings with sickness for years. It was difficult on them as well, trying to balance everything and not get emotionally involved. The concern for patients as people with feelings, as well as their fears, had probably caused these doctors to shed tears to the point that they had no tears of their own left to shed. This was a new and frightening experience for me. These doctors had dealt with this over and over again, and they had to keep focused on what they believed would help from a scientific point of view. But I am human and needed human interaction.

I felt like I was in line with multiple other cows being run through a squeeze shoot, and I was just the next cow in line. The lack of empathy present through this conveyor-belt process was difficult; yet, it was understandable since the doctors faced it every day.

Mark and I left this doctor's office, and I had to stop and think, "Well, this well-meaning doctor makes her living by performing surgery, breast surgery." I thought about it for a while; I am a business woman in sales, and if someone came to me and asked me if I thought they needed new furniture or flooring, I would respond, "Yes." So, I knew that I needed to wait. I still felt that there had to be another way. Mark and I determined to wait for the results of the PET scan before deciding what to do.

The PET Scan

~It seemed to be extremely dark this morning, the 18th of May, 2012; we had stayed the night at one of the hotels next door to the hospital since the PET scan was scheduled for 5:30 a.m.. We arrived earlier than my appointment time; I sensed an extreme feeling of loneliness as I picked up my cell phone, heart pounding, and called to let the hospital know we were outside. Since it was so early, the doors were locked, and the attendant had to come and open it up for us. Mark was with me, right at my side. We had been given a cell phone number to call and the name of the man who would answer.~

Oh, the thoughts I had to fight that day!

(For the weapons of our warfare are not carnal, but mighty through God to the pulling down of strong holds;) 5. Casting down imaginations, and every high thing that exalteth itself against the knowledge of God, and bringing into captivity every thought to the obedience of Christ; (II Corinthians 10:4-5)

I knew that I had to cast down imaginations. I had to keep meditating on the scriptures because I also knew that in Christ Jesus I had been provided everything I would ever need.

He sent his word, and healed them, and delivered them from their destructions (Psalms 107:20).

This was turning out to be the most trying time of my entire life; I knew that I could not allow my mind to focus on anything but what the word of God said about me. I had faith in my heart but doubt in my head. Shaking with fear, I was trying with everything in me to put the worry and fear of cancer down.

I picked up my phone and made the call. The man came to open the door, and we walked in. He took us through a series of doors and down several halls until we arrived in a room. They told Mark that he could not stay because the man administering the test was about to inject me with a sugar-based radioactive material that would attach itself to cancer in my body. At this time, I did not know that cancer's number one food is sugar, therefore, doctors use it in these tests. They told me that my body needed to stay calm throughout the next hour while I awaited the PET scan. I thought, "Oh, yes, that is an easy thing to do!" I really felt alone now; they wouldn't allow my husband in the room. They turned the lights off and told me to relax. I tried, but fought back tears and emotions that raged inside. Mark was out in the waiting room praying for me. It really made me appreciate Mark even more, knowing he cared so much.

I was allowed to listen to my iPod, and David Hogan, an evangelist, popped up. I had been listening to several of his sermons, so I listened to him as I felt a burning sensation hitting my body in many areas. I had to make myself meditate on the Word. After the hour was up, the door opened, and the man took me to the next room for the PET scan.

I arrived in a room with a huge machine and was instructed to lie down in the machine with my arms up over my head and not move for the next hour. It was a very difficult hour as pain ran through my body. I could really feel the pain in my sternum, back and left hip. I had been experiencing pain for years in those areas but never thought it was cancer. It was an incredibly long hour as my hands began to grow numb, and my back was beginning to hurt from lying down on the machine. What a relief when I heard someone say, "Five more minutes!"

When his voice came over the speaker and said, "Now you can move; I was so relieved!" I really tried to relax, but the battle in my mind had reached new levels. I felt pain in so many areas of my body during the injection and the PET scan. I began to move my arms, which were tingling from not being moved for an hour, not to mention that my arms had been raised up above my head. I had been experiencing so much pain for so long even if my arms were down, especially my right arm. Before the scan, the man was very nice and looked me in the eyes. After the scan, he wouldn't look me in the eyes. I asked him about the scan, and he replied, "I am not the doctor."

Now, the scan was over, so we left the Baylor Hospital in Plano, Texas, and headed home. I was so thankful to be going home. I do not like to be away from my family. The long, nine-hour drive proved to be a trial within itself as I dealt with thoughts trying to torment me with fear. I continually reminded myself that God has not given me a spirit of fear, leading to the realization that if God had not given me a spirit of fear, where did it come from? Well, you guessed it right – it comes from the thief, the deceiver himself, the devil and his demons! I knew I had to continue to fill myself with the Word of God: the truth that would set me free.

While driving home, we stopped every few hours to get out and walk; my left hip, my sternum and vertebrae were really hurting; I think it had to do with the injection for the scan. There were not many places to stop and eat on the road since my diet was very limited. I am so thankful for Jason's Deli having organic greens on the salad bar. We stopped in Abilene and that's what we ate, along with a bowl of vegetable vegan soup. Mark has been so helpful to encourage me, and he was even eating (for the most part) what I would eat. I had always eaten chicken and thought I was doing great by doing so. I later found out that the non-organic chicken I had been eating contained so much estrogen – due to mainstream chicken farmers in America feeding estrogen to their chickens to keep up with demand for chicken breasts. Estrogen makes the chickens' breasts develop quickly and thus increases the estrogen level in the bodies of all of us who consume the estrogen-laden chicken. That is one of the reasons, I believe, for the rise in cancer in children. I made a decision to only eat organic, free-range chicken, so I would stay clear of the estrogen.

~How wonderful it was to pull up to the house and see the kids and the animals. I was ready for the peace and quiet of home.~

Jesus Appears to Me.

~Well, neither Mark nor I have peace about any of the avenues that the doctors have suggested thus far; so, we went home to fast and pray.~

We arrived home last night, which was Friday. Saturday morning, May 20, 2012, I was in the kitchen wiping down my countertops, and Jesus appeared in our living room on the staircase, which is open to the kitchen. He didn't say anything, but I remembered that years before Jesus spoke to me at the same place he was now standing. I was woken up in the night sometime during the spring of 2005, hearing someone call my name, "Shirley!" Well, I got up and checked on Mark to make sure he was breathing (after all the years of being a medic, it seemed like the thing to do). I then proceeded to go and check on the three kids, who were all asleep in their beds. After a period of time, I went back to bed and fell asleep. A little while later, I was awakened again, " Shirley!" Someone was calling my name again. I got up and again checked on Mark, and he was still sound asleep; I then went on to check on all the kids again. I even turned the lights on to make sure that everything was okay. I checked the gas cooktop in the kitchen to make sure no burners were on and leaking gas. I went to the garage to check on things. I went out to the barn to check on our horses and chickens. Everything seemed to be fine. I couldn't figure out what was going on and why I was being awakened. I prayed and asked God to show me what it was that He was telling me. So, about an hour later, I went back to bed. Shortly after falling asleep, again, I heard, "Shirley!" I jumped up out of bed this time, grabbed my Bible, and went to the living room downstairs in my house and just sat before the Lord reading His Word. About an hour later, I got up to walk back up the stairs to the bedroom, and when I did, I heard the Spirit of the Lord speaking to me, and He said, *"Fear not: for I have redeemed thee, I have called thee by thy name; thou art mine. When thou passest through the waters, I will be with thee; and through the rivers, they shall not overflow thee: when thou walkest through the fire, thou shalt not be burned; neither shall the flame kindle upon thee; (Isaiah 43:1b,2)*

What a word -- He has called me by my name. I was excited in a way, but what about the passing through the water and walking through the fire reference? – that, I didn't quite understand at that moment. Now, I am seeing Jesus stand at the same place on the staircase, where he spoke to me years earlier. Things were starting to make sense: I knew what I was facing wasn't good; but, He had told me years earlier to "Fear not" and "He had called me by my name." There was hope: in the water, he would be with me, and the rivers wouldn't overtake me. Oh, and the fire? I wouldn't be burned! He promised! There was some sense of peace now, knowing this wasn't a surprise for my Lord.

Later that day, I laid down and went to sleep, praying in the Spirit. I was awakened early in the morning at 3:33 a.m., and Jesus was standing at the foot of our bed. I was in bed but now wide awake as I saw Jesus. I knew it was him; he had come and appeared to me on other occasions when I needed him. An incredible peace always accompanies him – and divine direction which always gave me hope. Every time he has appeared to me, there was never audible words, but he would speak to me with thought transfer. It was as if every question that I had about whatever I was going through he already knew every detail about the circumstance and had an answer that he transmitted to me through a knowing deposited inside of me.

In His manifested presence this physical world fades away and the reality of Him is more real than anything I have ever experienced on this earth.

He that hath my commandments, and keepeth them, he it is that loveth me: and he that loveth me shall be loved of my Father, and I will love him, and will manifest myself to him. (John 14:21)

At that moment, I looked at Jesus, and I felt something very unusual. I began to sweat behind my right knee. I said, "Lord, are you telling me to sweat?" He then disappeared. Oh, the peace that I was totally immersed in at the moment. Hope! I was so excited! I knew that I had been waiting to hear from heaven. I turned to my husband who was sound asleep and said, " Mark, Mark, wake up! Jesus just came and stood at the foot of the bed, and I think he told me to sweat; yes, I really think he just told me to sweat." I kept thinking, "Did he really just tell me to sweat?"

Later that Sunday morning before church, I had been pondering and praying about what I had received. Mark looked up in the scriptures and found every place where we could find the word, "sweat." I found myself being moved concerning where Jesus was in the garden, and He sweated as it were great drops of blood because of what he was facing, and He prayed more earnestly. So, we prayed more earnestly. (Luke 22: 43 & 44). I knew that nothing would take the place of hearing the still, small voice of God because I knew the words that He speaks are spirit and life:

Jesus had come. He had spoken to me, but what did it mean? I knew Jesus said:

It is the spirit that quickeneth; the flesh profiteth nothing: the words that I speak unto you, they are spirit, and they are life (John 6:63).

Telling the Church

~We got up this morning early and went to the church that we pastor in Alpine, Texas, Grace Christian Fellowship, May 20, 2012. We wrestled with how to share the news with the congregation.~

My family all sat on the front rows of the church: my sister, Cindy, and her husband, Greg, and their children; my cousins (Uncle Farris' and Aunt Susan's children) – Stephanie and Keith and their children, and Daniel and Rebekah and their children. They all stood, along with the church members, and said they would stand with me and support me in prayer and believe for a miracle from God. They were all guarding me because of the concerns of how bad my sternum and ribs had been hurting. Doctors were concerned about how brittle my bones may have been. My sister, Cindy, wouldn't let anyone hug me and that was very hard since I am a hugger.

My husband opened with the scripture in Ephesians 1:16 on how we are one with Christ in the fullness of God. He began to share that I had been attacked in my body; then, he handed the microphone to me.

I told the church my diagnosis. I shared by faith that this giant, like Goliath, would surely fall, just like Goliath did when David killed him. I confessed that I was using five stones like David, and I would do what I knew. I would not put on the armor of Saul but the armor of the Spirit (my sling-shot -- this was all I knew that really worked), and I would fight this giant with the weapons of the Spirit and do spiritual warfare. Cancer was a modern-day Goliath that had risen up against the armies of the living God. How dare that uncircumcised Philistine (cancer) come against the people of God! Jesus had already paid the price for my healing.

I told the church what the reports of the doctors were but that Jesus had stood before me early that morning with this directive: "Sweat." There was hope.

It was a precious day. I shared with the people, knowing that I had been strengthened.

I received a call from my father after church, and he had this scripture for me, the same day we were telling the church about my diagnosis.

And there appeared an angel unto him from heaven, strengthening him (Luke 22:43).

Little did my father know that I was pointed to the same exact scripture, as well as Luke 22:44, after Jesus appeared to me on this morning.

And being in an agony he prayed more earnestly: and his sweat was as it were great drops of blood falling down to the ground (Luke 22:44).

Over the days, weeks, and months to come, we found that many people did not stand with us. Many left the church, so many accusations came up against me. Some said that I was struck with cancer because I prayed for people and that it was punishment against me because it was not God's will to heal. Others spoke harshly against us and said that I had cancer because my husband allowed me to preach. Some sent cards and letters. I was so excited to receive the mail but then some were awful and very critical. I received a letter telling me to not believe God for healing -- that God did not heal anymore and I just needed to prepare to die and face reality. Wow! Was I ever shocked. It was hard enough for me to understand that people really thought some of those things; it was even harder for me to believe that they would say it. There was one person who went even to the point of wanting to debate with my husband while he was preaching. This person on a Sunday morning stated that God had predestined some to be sick and some to never receive salvation and that salvation and healing was not for everyone.

Well, there is a righteous indignation that rises up within me when people try to take away from what I know I have received as some clarity in the area of healing, and I know that it is God's will to heal and that it is God's will to save whosoever will call on the name of the Lord Jesus. He is not willing that any should perish but all to come to the knowledge of Jesus Christ as Lord and Savior. I do know that not all receive salvation and that not all receive healing, but the provision has been made. So, I made a decision to keep pressing in for more. I decided that if healing was for one and God was not a respecter of persons then it must be for me, too. I have prayed for many and have seen many healed; I have shared salvation and many have received salvation. I don't know everything, but I do know that God's Word is true. Just because we may not understand it all doesn't mean that we can begin to deal with situations based on our experience. We must stand on the Word of God. I remember hearing a minister say, "Faith begins where the will of God is known." I dove into the word of God more and more to discover His will, and my faith increased. The book of Ephesians jumped off the pages, and the truth set me free. The book of Colossians and the book of Romans all brought revelation as the Holy Spirit led me. I had to immerse myself in the gospels to hear of the good works of Jesus, being the express image of the Father God. Oh, I so wanted to know of Him more and the power of the resurrection. I know that we have to choose who we will serve. We have to choose whether or not we will fight the good fight of faith. We have to choose life so that we and our seed will live. Our weapons are not physical. It is not flesh and blood that we are warring against. There is a real enemy who wants to deceive us into thinking that it is not God's will to heal us. We empower the enemy with our thoughts, words, meditations and agreement. Our will has so much to do with everything, and our thoughts are much more important than most realize. I heard Doctor Caroline Leaf speak at a conference in Marathon, Texas, at the Gage Hotel, and she said, based on her studies, 97 % of all sickness and disease starts in the mind and that includes cancer. No wonder the Bible tells us to meditate on the Word of God, guard our hearts, have our minds transformed and cast down imaginations and bring every thought into agreement with God. The Bible tells us that we can't walk together with Him except we agree with Him (Amos 3:3). The Bible goes on to tell us that when there is unity God will command a blessing. Based on God's Word, I made a decision to come into total agreement with Him. After all these things that we had to walk through, we had to continue to forgive and hold no grudges against anyone. I will never forget the day that I was strengthened by an angel. Little did I know how much I would really need it.

The PET Scan Revealed the Cancer Had Gone Too Far!

Monday, the 21st of May, the day after Jesus came to me, I got up and went to work, anticipating the call from the doctor to go over the PET scan. After waiting for some time and not receiving a call from the doctor to go over the results, I decided to go ahead and call her instead. When the doctor got on the line, she began to go over the report from the PET scan and said, "Well, you have cancer in your breast, clavicle, sternum, ribs, front and back, your vertebrae (and listed all the places on my vertebrae), your endocrine system, your left pelvic bone, left ovary, pubic bone, and have a mass in your lungs." She continued, "Well, cancer is all over your body." My diagnosis was Stage 4 Cancer that had metastasized to my bones, lymph nodes, and organs.

I was in a state of shock and couldn't believe what I was hearing. She didn't have a good prognosis for me at all. Everything had changed from the first findings to now. I was told that I had about ninety days to live. I hung up the phone and my daughter, Shanee, who was there with me at the office, came over and hugged me as I wept and cried harder than I had ever cried in my life.

I picked up the phone and called my husband and told him the doctor's report. He began to speak life over me. He began to boldly declare the Word of God over me and to remind me that I was under a new and better covenant and that all the promises in Christ Jesus are "Yes" and "Amen" to me because I had entered into a new covenant relationship with Jesus when I believed on Him as my Lord; therefore, by His stripes we are healed — Wow! I really needed to hear that!

So far, I had been told many scriptures that encouraged me that God was there and to not be afraid; that this sickness would not bring my death, and, yet, all the doctors, ultrasounds, biopsies, scans, and tests had only brought me the sentence of death.

I was trying to stand on the Word of God and the promises of God, but death and fear stalked me like a hungry lion, and I was battling fear unlike any other time in my life and didn't want to die!

New Ultrasound Results

Early on the morning of May 23, 2012, I had another ultrasound when I got back to Dallas. The first PET scan showed cancer in my left ovary, so the doctor scheduled an ultrasound to get a better look at my ovary. We were sitting in the waiting room at the Baylor Hospital, and our cell phone rang. Mark answered the phone, and it was John G. Lake Ministries (ran by Curry Blake) calling to pray for me. Someone in our church had called them to ask for prayer. They began to speak life over me and definitely prayed a prayer of faith with my husband as the nurse came to call me back to the exam room. The technician looked at my paperwork and performed the ultrasound, and then she said, "I am not a doctor, but I do this all the time, and your ovary is clear. I don't see any cancer in your ovary." It felt like a ton of bricks fell off my shoulders, and I began to thank Jesus for the healing of my ovary and my entire body. Healing had already begun to manifest!

My treatment at Dr. June's still included me sitting in the sauna, but each time, it would take less and less time to break into a sweat. All of these tangible results so encouraged me as I continued to walk in faith.

"Sweat"

After leaving Plano, Texas, May 23, 2012, I had yet another appointment to see another oncologist, Dr. Olivares, with Texas Oncology in Garland, Texas, whom Dr. June Meymand, the nutritionist, wanted me to go and see. We had made an appointment for yet another opinion.

I had asked one of the other doctors with Texas Oncology about Dr. Olivares, and this doctor was very angry that I wanted to go and see another doctor. She spoke strongly against Dr. Olivares and said, "He thinks outside the box." She went on to say, "I don't even think he is still part of Texas Oncology." I was actually very excited to hear that because everyone else's thinking "inside the box" was not bringing me any hope.

When we arrived at his office for the visit, he looked over my records and told me, "According to medical science, you are terminal. At this stage, chemo and radiation will probably kill you." He said the cancer had advanced too far and was too wide spread throughout my body to treat me with chemotherapy and also went on to say that radiation if used would probably kill me too since the cancer was all over my body. He said surgery would just dismember me and not improve my quality of life or extend it. Then he paused and said, "But, we can believe God for a miracle." I was so relieved to hear some hope from an oncologist, and a miracle was something I could believe for!

Then he stopped and looked at me and said, "I have one word for you: I want you to sweat!"" Wow! I began to cry and cry. " How could this be?" I thought. This doctor just told me what Jesus told me three days ago. I knew this was where I needed to be. We shared with the doctor about Jesus coming to see me and speaking the same word to me just days before. I knew in my spirit that this was Jesus showing me the way to life.

He instructed me on what to eat and what foods to avoid. He also told me that he knew the cancer that hit my body was estrogen-fed, and he wanted to start me on an estrogen blocker, which he prescribed. I told him that I had been to see Dr. June Meymand at the Healing Arts Cancer & Wellness Center in Dallas, Texas. He encouraged me to do what she recommended and said that together we could believe God for a miracle.

Commanding My Body to Sweat

~May 23rd, after leaving Texas Oncology, our oldest daughter, Shatiel, and our granddaughter, Amalee, flew in from Florida to see me for a while. Shatiel and her husband, Adam Brant, are pastors in Florida. Recently, a woman in their church who was around my age had passed away from cancer. I am sure this was a grave concern to Shatiel. She came to encourage me and to help with the things at home.~

We drove to Dr. June's clinic, and I received the first toxin cleanse through a foot bath. She told me that she would allow me to go home for the weekend, but I had to be back at her clinic on Tuesday and would not be allowed to leave the clinic for ninety days.

Dr. June also put me in a sauna infused with concentrated oxygen and ozone. I sat in it for twenty-five minutes at 119 degrees, and I did not break a sweat. Mark came over to the sauna and spoke over me and commanded my body to release sweat; within minutes, I began to sweat.

Afterward, we drove to Cleburne to stay with my Uncle Farris and Aunt Susan for the night. It was nice to stay the night with them. The next morning, Aunt Susan showed me how to juice, and they sent us home with a juicer for me to use. I had always really enjoyed vegetables, and I liked the taste of the fresh vegetable juice. Aunt Susan cooked breakfast for us the next morning, and it was so good. After Dr. June had given me some direction on what to eat and what not to eat, it made eating out a little difficult. So, instead of eating something wrong, I just made a decision to not eat until something on my list was available.

We stayed the night at the Holiday Inn Express after leaving

Dr. June's, and I spent some time outside since it was such a warm day, trying to sweat. For years, I just wanted to stay comfortable and never thought about the importance of sweating; now, it was vitally important.

The next morning, we went to Baylor Plaza II in Garland, Texas, for a full-body nuclear bone scan. Shatiel and Amalee waited in the waiting room while I was being injected with some radioactive substance that would cause any cancer to show up. This machine was just as uncomfortable and very nerve racking. Constantly, I had to stay on top of my thoughts and emotions to not allow the enemy have a foothold in my life. After the nuclear bone scan, I returned to Dr. June's clinic for continuing treatments, a foot detox, sauna and a nutritional IV before leaving that day. Finally, we got to go home for the weekend. What a blessing! We drove to Abilene from Dallas and stayed the night at a Holiday Inn Express right off the interstate; we were all exhausted.

Speaking to the Cancer

For we wrestle not against flesh and blood, but against principalities, against powers, against the rulers of the darkness of this world, against spiritual wickedness in high places (Ephesians 6:12).

We felt we were to become more specific as to what I was facing and how we prayed in regards to it; we were in a battle for my life. We began to recognize that it was not flesh and blood that we were dealing with, according to Ephesians 6:12. We needed to see that this could indeed be something spiritual manifesting in the flesh.

When you have received Jesus as your Lord, your spirit man is born again. The demonic forces come against your soul (mind, will, and emotions). We must cast down imaginations and use the weapons we have been given to fight the good fight of faith.

For the weapons of our warfare are not carnal, but mighty through God to the pulling down of strongholds; Casting down imaginations, and every high thing that exalteth itself against the knowledge of God, and bringing into captivity every thought to the obedience of Christ; (II Cor 10:4-5)

I believe cancer is demonic, of the devil, because it comes to steal, kill and destroy. I believe that it is a spirit of infirmity manifesting in the flesh. I had always been the one to run after people that needed a touch from God and saw God do the miraculous over and over again. I have cast out demons; I have seen the dead raised. Now, I saw the enemy had come to steal, kill and destroy my life. Even in war times, the enemy wants to take out those that are taking down the enemy. The thief wanted me out of the picture.

And when he had called unto him his twelve disciples, he gave them power against unclean spirits, to cast them out, and to heal all manner of sickness and all manner of disease (Matthew 10:1).

The thief cometh not, but for to steal, and to kill, and to destroy: I am come that they might have life, and that they might have it more abundantly (John 10:10).

We felt we were to "speak to spirit of cancer." Call it by name.

There are many evil forces; hundreds trying to invade your body through the toxic world that we live in – preservatives in our food, sugar, additives, pesticides, unforgiveness, deep hurts, ***stress, not enough rest***, emotional wounds, broken hearts, broken relationships, traumatic events that lead to great disappointments, and discouragements. Some movies, along with some music that promote, anxiety, fear, panic, etc., could lead to open doors for the enemy.

*And he said unto them, **Take heed what ye hear:**...(Mark 4:24)*

I began to see that there are so many people looking for help, praying for healing and desiring to be healed, delivered, set free and restored, but because they have never allowed the Holy Spirit to do a work and heal them everywhere they hurt, they continued to have an open door for the enemy to stay. The thief has to have access for the power of the enemy to be active in our lives. When we close the door and quit allowing access to the enemy through forgiving, obeying (When the Holy Spirit says to rest, we need to rest.) and allowing our hearts and minds to be mended, the enemy ceases to have a foothold and has to leave. This thief, named cancer, had come to steal, kill and destroy my life: Jesus came to make a way out for me. The enemy is very real, and you must understand whom it is that is tormenting you.

Many times, I have found out that I could tell the "critters" (demon spirits) to come out of people, but they would be right back because the open door was there, and the legal access for the enemy has to be closed, shut off. I began to see how God had to heal my broken heart so that no sickness or disease (no unclean spirit) would have any right in my life. God began to deal with me about hurts and rejections that I had dealt with for many years that had to be mended. I began to speak the Word of God over my emotions and wounds and allow Him to heal me everywhere I hurt. The Holy Spirit opened my eyes and showed me that my entire life I had been performance-oriented, based upon deep-seeded hurts and wounds of rejection. He had come to heal me and bring restoration. I had received so much rejection, being a woman in ministry, and the Holy Spirit took me down a path of revelation knowledge that would change the way I thought and would bring me to a place of knowing, without a doubt, that Jesus had called me by my name. He showed me that in the kingdom of God there was neither male nor female and that I just needed to go into all the world and preach the good news just as he called me to do.

The Spirit of the Lord is upon me because he hath anointed me to preach the gospel to the poor: he has sent me to heal the brokenhearted, to preach deliverance to the captives, and recovering of sight to the blind, to set at liberty them that are bruised, To preach the acceptable year of the Lord (Luke 4:18-19).

THIS WOULD BE A TURNING POINT IN WHICH WE WOULD BECOME VIOLENT IN FIGHTING BACK!

And from the days of John the Baptist until now the kingdom of heaven suffereth violence, and the violent take it by force (Matthew 11:12).

Looking at this scripture was a revelation that there is a place where God rules and reigns, and the kingdom of heaven allows us to press into that place; those who are energetic towards pressing in to this place will seize the kingdom of heaven on earth, and the kingdom of God will be able to operate. Jesus said, "Thy kingdom come, and Thy will be done here on this earth as Your will is already done in heaven" (Matthew 6:10 paraphrased). Jesus would share with his disciples these truths that would change and transform all of us. We must see the importance of having our minds transformed to prove God's will here on earth.

And be not conformed to this world: but be ye transformed by the renewing of your mind, that ye may prove what is that good, and acceptable, and perfect, will of God (Romans 12:2).

We must put off the old way we have done things and be changed – transformed through our soul (mind, will, and emotions) being changed through the Word of God so that we can prove his will here on this earth.

That ye put off concerning the former conversation the old man, which is corrupt according to the deceitful lusts; 23. And be renewed in the spirit of your mind; 24. And that ye put on the new man, which after God is created in righteousness and true holiness (Ephesians 4:22-24).

Our son-in-law, Adam Brant sent me a link to a lecture by Dr. Caroline Leaf, a neuroscientist who had done extensive research on the brain. Her work opened my eyes to a new dimension of revelation as well as showing me an open door the enemy could use to steal, kill, and destroy our lives. Our brains were not made to meditate on the negative; we were created to think on the things that are good, honest and true and of good report.

Finally, brethren, whatsoever things are true, whatsoever things(are) honest, whatsoever things(are) just, whatsoever things (are) pure, whatsoever things (are) of a good report; if (there be) any virtue, and if (there be) any praise, think on these things (Philippians 4:8).

I highly recommend that you get Dr. Caroline Leaf's work and study it; it will change the way you think. Her website is www.drleaf.com.

Preparing to Stay Ninety Days in the Clinic

During the meeting my husband and I had with Dr. June, she looked at me with concern on her face and told me I may only have ninety days left to live. She explained that there was a possibility of keeping the cancer from spreading any further, and the positive effects of these changes may improve the quality of my life as well as even extend my life. Dr. June encouraged me to follow my doctor's treatment plan, and in the meantime, she would help me to stay as well as possible during my treatments.

The nutritionist explained how traumatic surgery is on the body. She explained that we did not want to breakdown my body any further; instead, we wanted to build my body up by maintaining my healthy cells enough to keep fighting the cancer.

The nutritionist was encouraging, but at the same time, she told me to deal with the facts, according to the options my doctors had placed before me. I valued her advice and considered it carefully, knowing that she meant well and had compassion for people.

I had much to consider at this time. I reflected upon the interlacing nature of my body, soul, and spirit. The power of words in the declaration of salvation floated to the forefront of my mind, knowing that it is with the heart that man believes and with the mouth confession is made unto salvation:

That if thou shalt confess with thy mouth the Lord Jesus, and shalt believe in thine heart that God hath raised him from the dead, thou shalt be saved (Romans 10:9).

The word salvation is not just for the spirit man; the word "salvation" in Greek is "sozo" which translates to "save, heal, and deliver." The word, sozo, comprises salvation for the whole man: spirit, soul, and body. I knew the principle of declaration of salvation must be applied to my life. I began declaring the Word of God over my body and speaking scriptures out loud over and over, not just words, but *faith-filled* words, not vain repetitions, but out of my heart and with my mouth. This is what Jesus said in Mark 11:23.

For verily I say unto you, That whosoever shall say unto this mountain, Be thou removed, and be thou cast into the sea; and shall not doubt in his heart, but shall believe that those things which he saith shall come to pass; he shall have whatsoever he saith.

Even as my husband and I traveled home to pack some things and prepare for me to stay at the clinic for the next three months, I kept surrounding myself with faith-filled teachings and filling my days with God's word. If I was not reading it, I was listening to the Word on CD.

When the pain became so overwhelming that I found it difficult to focus or read, I did more listening as I found it much easier to just listen, finding peace and encouragement through this time because I was hearing the Word of God. The Word says:

So then faith cometh by hearing, and hearing by the word of God (Romans 10:17).

My Nightmare

Just as my ordeal of going to doctors and having tests ran on my body was in full force, I dreamed a dream that was so real and vivid that I woke up shaking.

I dreamed that I was in a building, like our church that had a lot of glass on the front of the building. I saw a huge double-decker semi-truck, overloaded, that was driving very fast. It was the largest truck I had ever seen. The truck went out of control and headed right toward the building where I was. I began to scream and warn people to get out of the way. I grabbed some children, trying to get them to safety. But, the truck was still headed straight to where I was.

Just about the time it got close to us, I was calling on the name of Jesus. I kept calling out, "Jesus!, Jesus!" Then the truck flipped over on its side and was skidding right toward me. When it got to the building where I was, the truck stopped right up against the glass window that I was standing behind. The truck just barely tapped the window but did not break, not even a crack.

Then I heard a voice say, "This is the cancer that I just stopped." I woke up from this dream, shaken, and pondering it.

(I dreamed this dream while I was at Dr. June's clinic, just after a few days of being there, May 30, 2012.)

A Brutal Day at the Clinic

Like every day at the clinic, patients came for treatment. The despair and depression was overwhelming; some had already gone through surgery, radiation, and chemotherapy. So many people know little or nothing about Christ, His power and His promises, much less the forces of the demonic that are seeking whom they may devour.

Be sober, be vigilant; because your adversary the devil, as a roaring lion, walketh about, seeking whom he may devour: 9. Whom resist steadfast in the faith, knowing that the same afflictions are accomplished in your brethren that are in the world. 10. But the God of all grace, who hath called us unto his eternal glory by Christ Jesus, after that ye have suffered a while, make you perfect, establish, strengthen, settle you (I Peter 5:8-10).

At the clinic at night, I could hear a woman screaming out. This had happened several times; yet, there was no one else at the clinic except us at night. I asked the nurse, "Who stayed in the room where we were staying before us?" The nurse told me that a particular woman stayed there before us and that she screamed all the time because she was in so much pain. Finally, I decided it was a demon or a familiar spirit trying to bring fear on me, so I went through the clinic casting out this spirit and commanding it to cease to speak. (This ended the screaming spirit.)

And always, night and day, he was in the mountains, and in the tombs, crying, and cutting himself with stones (Mark 5:5).

For he said unto him, Come out of the man, thou unclean spirit (Mark 5:8).

I kept examining the tumors, and with each day that passed, they seemed to be getting smaller. The doctor had already given me an estrogen blocker since he had decided that this cancer was estrogen-fed and lived off of the estrogen and sugar in my body. We were starving the cancer!

The daily dose of vitamins was almost more than I could take. My chest hurt due to taking things I had never taken before. I had seldom taken even an aspirin or Tylenol and very few vitamins; yet now, I was taking a handful three times a day. It was sometimes hard to swallow that many vitamins. One day, it was especially difficult; I nearly choked to death as I tried to swallow them. I did not realize until later that there were tumors pressing against my esophagus from my sternum. After that, I made up my mind that I would not take the vitamins again without my husband or my daughter there to perform the Heimlich maneuver on me in case I choked again.

My food intake was vegetables and more vegetables. I have always loved vegetables, but now, I questioned myself, "Will I ever again love vegetables?" I was also eating very little meat.

~I have seen despair and hopelessness all around me – people in fear of death – yet I have hope in Christ:

(I had fainted, unless I had believed to see the goodness of the LORD in the land of the living (Psalms 27:13)).~

A Busy Lifestyle

I had always seemed to be so busy and really wouldn't have had it any other way. I just absolutely love the feeling of accomplishing something. My normal day was to get up early and cook breakfast for the family, which included my husband and me, our two children still at home, Shanee and Vaughn, and two twin boys, Kaden and Travin Silvers, who lived with us for a year. Then I would put lunch in the oven for whoever would be at home. We usually had an extra one or two for lunch, depending upon who came to work in our warehouse, where my husband does granite fabrication. Then it was time to throw something in the crock-pot for dinner to make sure everyone had something to eat. I love to cook and really enjoy preparing good meals for my family. I got that from my mother. She is an amazing woman and a very good cook, who always made sure we had something good to eat. With the schedule of our lives, sitting down together as a family to share a meal was always a very important time of day for everyone to come together and fellowship.

After the meals were well on their way, I would get ready and go to work. I drove thirty miles one way to work (I always looked forward to the drive time), then would be off to church to minister at a ladies' or youth meeting or visit a family, clean up the church, drive another thirty miles back home, clean up the kitchen, start the laundry, go through the mail, pay the bills, clean the house, fold laundry, figure out what I would cook for the next day, shower, read my Bible, then go to bed to sleep for a few hours. It was usually already into the morning hours by that time, but I could always get more accomplished during the midnight hours than any other time.

My father had been in the Marine Corps and believed strongly in working very hard and made sure none of his children were lazy. He always encouraged us to do it all – to not settle for the easy road. He stressed to work harder, do more, accomplish more, that we could handle it, and so we did. No one pushed me like I did. I had two brothers and a sister, and when we were growing up, we were always competing against each other. Everything was a challenge for me, and since I wanted the best grades in school, I pushed to be the hardest worker. I always wanted to do more than anyone else and to be a blessing to others and give them a break. I had a hard time asking people for help: a real type-A personality!

My Visitation of Jesus at Thirty-Three Years of Age

I think back to a very special birthday when I turned thirty-three years old, a day I will never forget. It is still as fresh in my memory as if it just happened.

On my birthday, at three o'clock in the morning, Jesus came to me. This was not in a dream. He came and stood in my room and turned to walk down the hallway. I got up and followed Him. He walked to the end of our hallway and then passed through a door as though it was not even there; I reached to grab the door knob to open the door and follow Him, and when I did, He spoke to me and said, "The day that my ministry here on earth ended will be the day that yours begins." Then He was gone.

I was very moved and thought about this a lot; I knew that Jesus was thirty-three at the time of his death, burial, and resurrection.

It had been a week prior that I had a dream in the night, and I was spoken to and this is what I heard:

You have not chosen me, but I have chosen you, and ordained you, that ye should go and bring forth fruit, and [that] your fruit should remain: that whatsoever ye shall ask of the Father in my name, he may give it you (John 15:16).

~Both of these events are back to back within a short time, and now, my spirit man is very inquisitive as to what does all of this mean?~

After That Visitation

For years after this visitation, I studied the Word earnestly. I shut off all music and only listened to teaching and read the Word. I couldn't get enough, for a hunger had ignited within me. I spent more time in prayer and fasting than ever before. I began to have a compassion for the sick and noticed the sick, crippled, and lost everywhere I went. I would run to people to pray for them with an inferno burning within me by the Holy Ghost.

One day I was praying, and I asked the Lord why I had not seen any blind eyes opened, and He asked me, "Well, how many blind eyes have you prayed for?" I paused and knew that I had not been praying for the blind, but I soon began. I prayed for so many people who were blind and did not see anyone healed; but I kept on, knowing that God's Word is true.

I began to examine myself, my heart, and my intents. I received a revelation one day while stepping out of the shower.

It came so clear to me that we were to "love God with all our heart, soul, mind, and strength and love our neighbor as ourselves, and on these two commandments hung all the law and the prophets (Matthew 22:37,39,40)." I then heard, "the laws of sowing and reaping, the laws of prosperity, and the laws of healing." I grabbed my Bible and read these scriptures and read the verses in other translations. I saw that the very foundation that we needed for God to build upon was that of loving God and loving people. Without loving God and loving people, there was nothing. I began to be attentive as to how I treated people. It had always been my practice to treat people well, but the Holy Spirit was leading me into a new dimension of love.

One day, a difficult customer came in to my store. I was nice to them, but when they left, I breathed a sigh of relief and rolled my eyes. *No one saw me, I thought.* Then I heard the voice of the Holy Spirit say, "I saw that."

I immediately repented and asked God to forgive me. I so wanted to be used of God. I never wanted to displease Him. This began my journey of being more attentive to my thoughts, attitudes, emotions, and responses to others, walking in a new level of integrity in which I would be led and guided by the Spirit in every area of my life. Simultaneously, I began to see more miracles, healings, and restorations, and yes, even the blind eyes began to open. This level of integrity with God, even when no one else was looking, caused an amazing reaction, where the gifts of the Spirit began to flow so easily. I saw a greater love walk, and a greater love of God was now able to flow out of me. Mark and I began to see our finances were also affected by our love walk; everything was connected.

Words of Encouragement

Signs of Encouragement continued to come our way. We got up one Sunday morning and went to Gateway Church in Frisco, Texas. The associate pastor, Stephen Gilbert, said he had a word for us. (This pastor had never seen us and did not know us.) He said, "This is No Sweat for God," as he prayed for Mark and me.

Later in the week, I was really struggling, and I had cried off and on all week, just trying to cope with so many things. The thoughts from the enemy continuing to come at me. I continued to pray and speak the word of God aloud, but it was a struggle. Mark had rented two movies from Redbox, and we put the first one on to watch. The woman in the movie died of cancer, and the family moved and bought a zoo. Well, Mark was trying to get me to laugh, instead, I cried. Then within the first few minutes of the next movie, the person was also diagnosed with cancer and died; well, this wasn't turning out well. We shut off the movies and went to bed. The next day, still dealing with so many thoughts, I continued to go around and speak the word of God over myself aloud; When I turned on the television in the living area of the clinic, there was Kenneth Copeland, and he said, with his voice raised, "You're not going to die! Whose report are you going to believe, the doctor's or God's?" and my spirit leaped within me. I began to praise God and thank Him for the provision of healing for my body, and I knew that I knew that I knew that I would walk out of this whole and well. I really appreciated the body of Christ, especially now. Kenneth and Gloria have always been living testimonies to me of faith-filled lives.

Another day, I watched Joel Osteen, and he was speaking in the same realm of truth. It was always encouraging and refreshing to my spirit to watch Joel Osteen. I knew that his mother had been diagnosed with liver cancer, and God healed her. I had even read her book, which greatly encouraged me. She told how their church prayed for her and that she kept her mind on the Word and kept busy as much as she could in the church and praying for others, believing that God was her source and her healer. I knew that God was no respecter of persons, and what He did for her, He would do for me.

Many have said that "Faith begins where the will of God is known."

But without faith it is impossible to please him: for he that cometh to God must believe that he is, and that he is a rewarder of them that diligently seek him (Hebrews 11:6)

And this is the confidence that we have in him, that, if we ask any thing according to his will, he heareth us: and if we know that he hear us, whatsoever we ask, we know that we have the petitions that we desired of him (I John 5:14-15)

...lord, if thou wilt, thou canst make me clean...and Jesus put forth his hand, and touched him, saying, I WILL; be thou clean (Matthew 8:2-3 emphasis mine).

Bone Infusion

On another visit to the oncologist, he told me that my bones were weak and very fragile; he said they were like those of an old lady. Because my bones were weak, the cancer had gone where there was a breakdown; we needed to strengthen my bones. He encouraged me to take Zometa treatments that would help strengthen my bones. I was not at peace with this but felt that maybe this would help. I told my husband that I had not been directed by the Holy Spirit to take this; however, I would go ahead with the treatment.

While waiting for my very first bone infusion, I sat next to a woman who had been to see the doctor after my first visit. She had already gone through surgery and had been given her first round of chemotherapy. The doctor had told her that her hair would fall out in ten days. I began to share the Word of God with her and give her scriptures, and she began to write them down. This woman was so sweet. Asking her who her doctor was, I found out that it was the same doctor who wanted me to take chemotherapy and radiation treatments. This truly brought the realization home that except for the voice of God, I would have walked down the same road.

While I was getting this bone infusion, I was reminded of a movie about Corrie Ten Boone, *The Hiding Place*, in which one lady escaped while others were taken to the gas chamber. Fear was so strong and heavy that I had to make myself stay focused on the Word. The nurses brought in a woman, who had already lost her hair, into the same room where I sat. Slumped in a wheelchair, she was waiting for her next round of chemotherapy. She looked tired and very weak and did not have enough strength to even sit up straight.

Depression was overwhelming; my only escape was to open my mouth and begin to share hope with those around me. Everywhere I looked, I was staring death in the face.

After leaving the treatment room, we returned to the clinic. Not feeling well, I was experiencing a side effect from the bone infusion. I started running a fever and had chills, so I went and sat in the sauna for forty minutes at 120 degrees but did not break a sweat; I couldn't even get warm. I kept praying in the Holy Ghost. Mark came and helped me out of the sauna, almost carrying me to bed. Finally, around ten o'clock that night, my fever broke. It broke twice that night, and then I started feeling like I was coming back.

"I Want You to Enjoy Life!"

~The Holy Spirit was speaking to me this morning, I could hear, "Shirley, I want you to enjoy life."~

I began to cry as I heard this, for all of my life was all about working hard and getting plenty accomplished, but enjoying life was not really something that I considered. I was like a soldier, walking through every day doing what I believed was my duty. I had come to a place where day-to-day life was very difficult, and I had not been feeling well for so long that it was hard to even make it through a day, much less "enjoy" the day. I had been struggling with thoughts of not even wanting to continue to live because I felt like I was under so much stress and had so many people pulling on me from every direction. I just wanted to run away, but I was too responsible to do that. I loved the church, and it was the vision God had given to us, as we began with a small home bible study and had now purchased a 40,000 square foot building. but now, it was hard for me to even get up and get to church. I felt overwhelmed at times, even though I had always been up for a challenge. I cried out to the Lord many days as I drove home and asked Him to change things because I did not know how I could continue to live the way I was going. Things that I had previously enjoyed, I now hated; I did not know what was taking place on the inside of me. I kept asking myself what was going on with me, and why I was feeling this way. I struggled to stay awake even driving home and found myself requiring more sleep, but fighting against it because I never wanted to appear lazy.

I was reminded of a dream that I had years ago. In the dream, I was taken to a beautiful place where Jesus showed me his beautiful trees and gardens. I was so excited to see this place. He did not ever speak; it was like I knew what he was thinking, and he knew what I was thinking, like thoughts being transferred. When I looked at the trees and was so excited to see how beautiful they were, the trees began to move and sway, like they were dancing. He pointed me to the stars, and I looked, and I was so excited; when he saw that I was so excited, he made the stars twinkle for me and shine even brighter, like he was so happy that I enjoyed what he made. I then heard, "and for thy pleasure, they are created". I awoke from that dream and thought, that was so unusual, but I knew that the Holy Spirit was revealing to me that he wanted me to enjoy life, but I could not figure out how to stop long enough to look around, much less smell the roses.

Dreamed of a Girl Being Raised from the Dead

June 6, 2012 ~I dreamed of a girl being raised from the dead. It was as if we were on a mission trip and at church at the same time. Mexican food was being prepared like we serve at the church on Wednesdays after the youth service, and it seemed like the lady who helped me cook at church was cooking in the kitchen, even though I could not see her.~

I dreamed that a girl had been hurt on her right side, foot, leg, and other areas, and then she died. We buried her, and after the funeral, I went to check on things. I began to wipe the dirt away from the girl's face, and I began to call upon Jesus as I lifted her head and began to clean her up; then, she started moving her eyes. I saw the eyes open, but they were white. Then her eyes rolled, and she opened them and began to breathe and move. I continued to say, "Jesus, Jesus, Jesus, Jesus!" and I picked her up. Not only was she alive and breathing, but I could barely see the places where her right leg was hurt and cut previously; it was healed with only a small scar. She was whole and alive!

I woke up and felt the dream was about me. God was raising me up alive and whole. Jesus is my healer and my deliverer.

My Grandmother

A few years ago, my grandmother came to visit us for a few weeks. I woke up early to go check on her, and while approaching the door, I could hear my grandmother praying. It was around four in the morning, and I sat outside the door listening as Grandma prayed for each one of her children by name along with their children and grand-children and so on, with every person being named. I was so touched to hear her pray for each one of us, in order from the oldest to the youngest. When she named each child, I noticed that with each child or grandchild or great-grandchild she would wait on the Holy Spirit to move upon her to intercede for that family member. This so moved me that day that I was forever changed. Over the next few weeks following this experience, we prayed in the Holy Ghost daily. My grandmother, Virgie Whitehead, raised her children to serve God. Her daughter, my mother, had conveyed the message of salvation to me in a soft spirit. All of my mother's family had been raised in church and had either married preachers, become pastors, or worked in the church; indeed, I had a foundation to stand upon. It is no doubt why we are all here today – alive and serving God. I remember that when she exited her room that day, I leaned over to hug and kiss her and thank her for raising a household of faith.

I woke this morning, and Mark and I had been praying off and on through the night for Grandma – that she would not suffer, but she would leave this earth quickly and enter into glory. She had asked me two weeks ago to pray for her. After ninety-four years, Grandma was tired and ready to pass on from this life to "life more abundantly."

~June 7, 2012, Grandma went home to walk on streets of gold this morning

around 2:30 a.m.. We will all get to see her again one day. She was a mighty woman of faith!~

We had her funeral the following Monday morning at ten at Eastern Heights Church in Cleburne, Texas. There was a gathering of all eight of her children, her grand-children, her great-grandchildren and her great-great grand-children. What a glorious celebration. All of her children participated in the funeral in one way or another. I was so thankful to be a part of a household of faith. I spoke at her funeral and shared about the time that Grandma came and stayed with us as I sat outside her door as she prayed. I will never forget my Grandma, what a woman of God!

Meanwhile Back at the Church

The ladies at our church had begun to come together to pray for me. They knew what I was facing with a diagnosis of Stage 4 Cancer. Some worked in the medical field, and others had family members who had experienced cancer. No one had a good report or expectation after the cancer had progressed to Stage 4. Several had researched breast cancer on the internet and what they saw shocked them; I was already in shock.

This group of ladies, led by Betty Jones, came together at the church every morning to pray against the cancer. Betty was also connected to other groups of ladies in other cities who were intercessors. When difficult obstacles arose, Betty would call for the other intercessors to come together and pray. She called them together to pray for me. Betty sensed an urgency and unction of the Holy Spirit that everyone who was able would come to the church, so they could pray in power and unity. This was also done by conference calls of prayer over the phone.

Her call was answered, and many ladies came, either driving or flying in from many cities, to join with her in prayer. They had preceded this gathering with several days of fasting and praying in the Holy Spirit. This was such a key for the unity of purpose and the passion of focus.

These women of faith came together in the church every day while I was in the clinic in Dallas. They gathered around an empty chair, praying and directing their faith toward God, who knows no distance or time. When they had finished their time of prayer, they all agreed in faith that they had received the answer. The power of sickness and disease had been broken. The power of the enemy had to go along with tormenting spirits in the name of Jesus, and now, they expected the answer to come speedily.

They flew back to their homes. These great women of faith had carried their own expenses (transportation, food, and lodging); yet, they came anyway. Some came from Houston, San Antonio, Corpus Christi, Bay City, El Campo, Palacios, Fort Worth, Sandia (all in Texas), and Santa Fe, New Mexico. Their great effort would not be in vain. Also, Bible study groups within other churches were contacted to pray. Intercessors were expecting a miracle!

I could not find a record of their names, but they are all known by God for He sent them!

Betty called on some of the ladies in the church to come and begin to pray against cancer, calling it by name and commanding it to leave. This went on for several weeks. Several meetings of these ladies saw a mighty manifestation of the power of God being manifested over all the power of the enemy, with several people being saved and delivered within the church and our city.

These prayer times were not ordinary meetings but rather were dynamic in prayer and unction in the Holy Spirit.

Rebuking a Spirit of Fear!

I knew my assignment was to stay in the Word and meditate on the Word, and I also knew a spirit of fear had been trying to attack me.

On Tuesday, May 29, 2012, Mark and I went to visit a man who had been taking treatments at the clinic. The doctor that was caring for him wanted to do another round of radiation; the cancer was in his brain. After the radiation treatment, he went into a coma, and a short time later, he died. His wife came in crying and crying. I tried to comfort her, but at the same time, I was rebuking a spirit of fear trying to come against me. This man was only fifty-five years old.

~I could barely eat tonight, and it was hard to swallow. I know it was nerves from dealing with the man's wife today. I feel so much compassion for her. They are preparing for the funeral service.~

My parents called me and said, "Shirley, you are not there to pray for everyone and try to handle their problems. You are there to rest, be in a peaceful environment, and get well." They had no idea what I was going through, the day to day pressure was overwhelming, and I had never seen so many sick people. I had always prayed for almost every sick person I came in contact with. I knew we had been given power over all the power of the enemy. I had been shaken to the very core of my being, and believe me, my faith was being tested.

I am so thankful for my support system that is surrounding me daily. I receive text messages from the intercessors encouraging me and giving me words they have received for me that day. The messages continue to show up at the right time and what a boost to stay focused. Greater is He that is in me than he that is in the world.

I confess: Jesus took ALL my pain, ALL my sickness, and by His stripes, I AM HEALED!

I remember when Jesus came to me a week before my thirty-third birthday and spoke a scripture to me:

Ye have not chosen me, but I have chosen you, and ordained you, that ye should go and bring forth fruit, and that your fruit should remain: that whatsoever ye shall ask of the Father in my name, he may give it you (John 15:16).

I felt like I was hanging on for dear life, trying to control every situation, like I was hanging on to monkey bars, and when I couldn't hang on anymore, the Holy Spirit seemed to say to me, "Shirley, let go and I will catch you."

I knew that I needed to be free from a false sense of responsibility and from feeling that I needed to take care of everyone else. I tried to do so much on my own, always thinking that I was depending on God, but in reality, I was relying upon my strength and abilities as well. This would result in a time of dying to self and self-reliance. I humbled myself in a new dimension, knowing that only in Him was my hope and faith.

My Daily Routine

~I keep reminding my soul (my mind, will, and emotions) every day at the clinic that everything will be fine. I feel healing being manifested in my body.

My breast and nipple look better every day. The bruises from the biopsies are fading, almost gone. I can feel the tumors shrinking every day, and my hip, back, and sternum are feeling better too.~

I have a daily routine, not necessarily in this order that I believe is helping me:

- Eat breakfast, usually two scrambled organic eggs and a bowl of steel-cut oats.
- Juice four carrots, one beet, one cucumber, and one ice cube of wheat grass juice.
- Exercise: 30-60 minutes a day.
- Sauna: 30-40 minutes at 135 degrees (2 times a day.)
- Receive one nutritional IV, 30-45 minutes a day. (The nutritionist told me that many people who die from cancer actually die of starvation because they don't feel like eating properly and lack understanding of how to give the body the nutrients it needs.)
- Detox foot bath with IonSine Wave. This aids in pulling toxins from my body, 30 minutes a day.
- Sit in the sun at least 30 minutes a day (to absorb vitamin D for my bones and skin).
- RIFE Machine: 15-40 minutes twice a week, depending on the day and the setting. This machine disturbs the frequencies in cancer.

- Cook three organic meals a day from scratch.
- Take a handful of vitamins and minerals three times a day.
- Drink a shake of ½ avocado, ¼ cup yogurt, ¼ tsp. calamari oil, ¼ cup coconut milk, ¼ cup of kefir, 1 tsp. of flaxseed oil, and a scoop of instant protein.
- Drink natural blood thinner, this is something Dr. June made.
- Drink supplement: Intra Max, one ounce before noon.
- Take a magnesium supplement before bed each night with calcium, K2, and vitamin D.

Then Came the Vitamins

~Upon arriving at the clinic, Dr. June wanted me to take supplements. Well, I had taken a few vitamins over the years, but a cup of vitamins was now before me. I hardly believed I could swallow that many, much less keep them down. Dr. June had insisted I get the vitamins down, and if I threw them up, I was to take them again.~

I was already in such a weakened physical condition that even taking vitamins was difficult; yet, over the days, I began to increase in strength. It was like I could see a small spark of light at the end of the tunnel.

The body scan had shown my body was eaten up with cancer, in the four quadrants of my breast, my lymph nodes, sternum, clavicle, vertebrae (several), left ovary, lungs, hip, and pubic -- pelvic areas. In fact, the doctor told me, "It is easier to tell you where you don't have cancer than where you do because it has spread all over your body and is in your bones."

Could such things as sweating, foot baths, vitamins, and eliminating food additives and preservatives from the diet have the power to turn back such a devastating disease as what had locked on to me?

Based on everything I had been taught all my life, the answer was plain.

~The words that surrounded this field of modern, alternative medicine from those who oppose it are "quackery" and "snake oil." Yet, here I am, with nowhere else to turn, and I am seemingly getting a tiny bit better every day. Time will certainly tell: a new full-body scan and blood work has been set for the end of August, which will be the end of the ninety-day time frame I was given to live.~

Rest for a While.

~I heard this today, not audibly, but just in my spirit when I woke: "Rest for a while. Prepare to run again."

As of today, I have been at the clinic for a few weeks, and I have lost seven or eight pounds, and I didn't have much weight to lose; at least, I thought. I feel much better today than I did three weeks ago. I have been thinking about this scripture:

This book of the law shall not depart out of thy mouth; but thou shalt meditate therein day and night, that thou mayest observe to do according to all that is written therein: for then thou shalt make thy way prosperous, and then thou shalt have good success (Joshua 1:8).

It is so important that I pray without ceasing:

Pray without ceasing (I Thessalonians 5:17).

I have been praying in the Holy Ghost more than I ever have before. My mind is also so much sharper now.~

About a year or two ago, I began to notice that I couldn't recall some names that I should have known or just couldn't remember things I had always known. I had no idea this was all connected to an imbalance in my body and a disease raging inside.

The nutritionist gave me a list of supplements to take daily to get my body back in balance. This entire ordeal has made me very attentive to a balanced diet, and I have seen the importance of it in a new realm. I had been having a hard time swallowing all the supplements, but I kept making myself take them, even throwing them up at times and making myself go after them again.

I could not allow myself to ever come into agreement in my heart with what the doctors said concerning my death.

I took and pressed into the Word, being sensitive to the Holy Spirit's leading, guiding, and comforting me every step of the way:

~I am not jumping ship!~

And it shall turn to you for a testimony (Luke 21:13).

~I will surely give my testimony of what Jesus has done for me.~

And they overcame him by the blood of the Lamb, and by the word of their testimony; and they loved not their lives unto the death (Revelation 12:11).

(As it is written, I have made thee a father of many nations,) before him whom he believed, even God, who quickeneth the dead, and calleth those things which be not as though they were (Romans 4:17).

~I declare over my body that I am healed; I am whole; I am well; and I am restored! I am so thankful for the complete work that Jesus did for me on the cross.~

Don't Get in the Black Car!

~I am feeling that I am at a turning point inside; I feel better. I have been praying in tongues more and more every day.

I had a dream last night that I was walking on a sidewalk, and as I came to the end of the sidewalk, a black car came beside me to pick me up. The car was so close that I felt I could have touched it, but I knew I was not to get in the car. I turned around and went to the other side of a building, knowing I could walk through it.

Then, I was in a large building, and when I entered there were many people in it, and they came to see me bringing fabric or pieces of cloth, throws for sofas, dish towels, handkerchiefs, etc., anything that could be taken to the sick or unsaved. I knew in the dream I was walking in a new and different anointing. I knew people were being healed of all manner of sickness and all manner of diseases.

There was a rose that had been cut, and it was dried up, and the leaves around the rose were all withered. I reached down to pick it up, and the rose came alive again, and the greenery around it was renewed. I took the rose and stuck it in the dirt, which was very wet. Then, I woke up.~

We came home from church, and our bedroom and bathroom smelled like an abundance of roses – Jesus is the Rose of Sharon! I then remembered my dream of the rose.

There was cause for another celebration that day as well. Mark and I went to Gateway Church for the early service on June 10, 2012, the morning after this dream,, and when I went in, I had to go to the restroom. When I entered, I saw a girl. She said she was not feeling well, and then a word came to me for her, a very clear word about her life and what God had been dealing with her about. I told her that she had to repent, turn her life around, and quit rejecting the voice of the Holy Spirit. I also knew that Satan wanted to keep her from that service, for God had great things in store for her today. I prayed for her, and she felt better at that moment.

I left and went inside the church. She came in from another direction and sat down beside me. She received the baptism in the Holy Spirit at the end of the service, and I was able to walk forward with her and encourage her. What a precious time for a sixteen-year-old young lady!

"It's Not Over Yet!"

My father had received a word to warn me to be careful and only talk as the Holy Spirit unctions me. Talking before the Spirit tells me to speak is not wise.

And the king of Israel answered and said, Tell him, Let not him that girdeth on his harness boast himself as he that putteth it off (I Kings 20:11).

Go to now, ye that say, To day or to morrow we will go into such a city, and continue there a year, and buy and sell, and get gain: 14. Whereas ye know not what shall be on the morrow. For what is your life? It is even a vapour, that appeareth for a little time, and then vanisheth away. 15. For that ye ought to say, If the Lord will, we shall live, and do this, or that. 16. But now ye rejoice in your boastings: all such rejoicing is evil (James 4:13-16).

Let your words be few. Speak only the words that the Holy Ghost speaks to you, "Rhema Words."

~Do not boast about how far along you are or that the treatment is good. Don't speak of those things until it is over.

Today is the birthday of my only grandchild, June 12, 2012, Amalee Brant. She is one year old today. We were able to spend a little time with her via Skype on my computer.

I swam some today, about 13-14 minutes. I haven't felt good today and was very tired. I have been listening to the Word a lot and reading, especially the book of John.

I must stay focused. I must hear the voice of God.~

Get Equipment and Go Home!

~I was awakened at 3 a.m.. I received a message on Facebook from a brother in Christ named Jesus (we call him Jesse). I got up and walked through the clinic and checked on the children – they had come for a few days to spend time with me – and prayed in the Holy Ghost, meditating on the Word. ~

(My spirit man never sleeps but is praying without ceasing.)

I asked the Lord what He wanted me to do; was He speaking to me about any area, or did I need to pray for my children? I got up and dressed, and then heard someone in the clinic.

Dr. June had arrived early this morning, and we talked for a while. The best thing she said was, "If you get the equipment, I can teach your daughter to give you the IV's, and you can go home and do the therapy at home." That means I would not have to stay at the clinic for the last thirty days of treatment. That was music to my ears.

I knew that my Father God, Jesus my Lord, and the precious Holy Spirit would help me get the equipment.

The Still, Small Voice

~I woke up early around 4 a.m., praying in the Holy Ghost. I began to pray for every one of our children, our parents, my brothers, my sister, and all their families.

Driving home today (June 17, 2012) to Marathon. Mark will preach in the morning: "Sons of God can expect to hear from God; for as many as are led by the Spirit of God, they are the sons of God." I pray, "God, I want your purposes in my life. I don't want to miss you."~

And he said, Go forth, and stand upon the mount before the LORD. And, behold, the LORD passed by, and a great and strong wind rent the mountains, and brake in pieces the rocks before the LORD; but the LORD was not in the wind: and after the wind an earthquake; but the LORD was not in the earthquake: 12. And after the earthquake a fire; but the LORD was not in the fire: and after the fire a still small voice (I Kings 19:11-12).

An Attack of Pain!

~June 18, 2012, Driving back to Dallas: It was very hard to leave the kids and return to Dallas. There is not much that I can eat on the road. So, Jason's Deli it is again since it has an organic salad bar, where I can at least eat a salad.

I drove today, approximately half of the way. We had to stop along the way for me to walk. Since I am on Tamoxifen, a hormone to block estrogen in my body, I get out and move to keep up my circulation (one side effect of this estrogen blocker is blood clots).

I listened to Kenneth Hagin, Sr., all day while traveling. What a father of faith! He reminds me so much of my dad.

I opted to not take Coumadin (a blood thinner) but am taking a natural blood thinner that Dr. June prepared. She calls it natural medicine.

I am praying in the Holy Ghost and listening to Kenneth Hagin, and I am being attacked physically. I have been trying to read the Bible but just can't focus due to the pain, so it is easier for me to just listen right now. I know the enemy was trying to come back on me. I keep praying in the Holy Ghost. My breasts hurt, both breasts this time! Excruciating pain is running down my right arm and into my back, my sternum, my left hip, and my left ovary.

I continue to speak more: SPEAKING, YELLING, COMMANDING PAIN TO LEAVE IN THE NAME OF JESUS!! I yelled, "Jesus took my pain and all my sickness, and by His stripes, I AM HEALED!"

But he was wounded for our transgressions, he was bruised for our iniquities: the chastisement of our peace was upon him; and with his stripes we are healed (Isaiah 53:5).~

~I am so thankful for the Word which God sent to heal me and deliver me from my destruction~

He sent his word, and healed them, and delivered them from their destructions (Psalms 107:20).

~I am speaking the Word over my body. I have lots of pain today, but I have stayed focused on the Word.

It has been very difficult lately. I have had so much pain, even trying to go to the bathroom. When I would try to use the restroom, my left side would hurt so bad around my hip area and internally; I feel like there is some severe blockage, but I am speaking to the mountain to be removed.~

For verily, I say to you, that whosoever shall say unto this mountain, Be thou removed , and be thou cast into the sea; and shall not doubt in his heart, but shall believe that those things which he saith shall come to pass; he shall have whatsoever he saith (Mark 11:23).

~The pain broke about 10:33 p.m.. I continued to pray in tongues all day. It is a decision of my will to stay in the Word, even though it is difficult at times. Greater is He that is in me than he that is in the world.~

Buying the Equipment

~June 11, 2012, we buried Grandma; the service was held at Eastern Heights Church in Cleburne, Texas. She was buried in Cresson Cemetery beside Grandpa's grave.

Eastern Heights Church gave us an offering to help with our medical expenses today, and I was so overwhelmed with emotions. We had always been the ones to give and help; it was very different being on the receiving end. But, I praise God for His faithfulness and provision.~

We researched places to purchase equipment for therapy and were able to purchase the equipment with great help from family, friends, and the church.

We researched online for all the equipment we needed. We found the oxygen concentrator and ozone machine and purchased it from a company in Canada. And, we also found an infrared sauna in Kansas that we needed. The total sauna set up with oxygen concentrator and ozone cost $5,000.

We received a call back (finally) from a man with the IonSine Wave Foot Detox machine who said it would cost us $2,550. I called my mother, and she wired the money to him to rush the order. Praise God for help, great help!

Eastern Heights Church had given us an offering from their missions fund to help us with medical expenses, and we used all this to purchase equipment, so I could go home.

The RIFE Machine, a machine that disturbs the frequency of cancer, was purchased from a man in Florida. The cost was $2,500.

We were even able to find a used pedicure chair from a used furniture warehouse for $300.

The total cost of the equipment and shipping was about $10,300.

The average cost personally came to $11,000 a month for the first few months, and then gradually, the costs decreased when I was able to go home. This was over and above what my insurance had paid out for tests.

Before this would be over, the cost would exceed $50,000 paid by Blue Cross, our insurance provider, mostly for cancer tests. An additional cost of more than $100,000 for the clinic stay, the IV's, medicine, vitamins, and organic foods was paid by our family, friends, and church members.

Blue Cross would have paid $1,000,000 — if needed — but not for the nutritional, holistic direction I chose over the traditional treatment of surgery, chemotherapy, and radiation. Insurance did not cover one dime for what was restoring me to health.

How did I stand up to this expense? I had family, friends, and church. I readily admit that I had more than most to face this. What if I had not had so much more than others? I personally knew that God alone had made the difference; yet, I want to address this on behalf of all those other women who faced the overwhelming costs of medical treatment or as in my case alternative treatment.

The first thing I found necessary was to receive direction from the Holy Spirit. If He directs you in one direction over another, He will provide for that direction.

And Peter answered him and said, Lord, if it be thou, bid me come unto thee on the water. 29. And he said, Come. And when Peter was come down out of the ship, he walked on the water, to go to Jesus (Matthew 14:28-29).

You, too, can walk over anything when you know you are directed. First, find His will concerning what He directs you to do, no matter what it costs. If you know He tells you to do something, He will give you the faith to believe for every need. I read a book by F. F. Bosworth,

Christ the Healer. This book was extremely instrumental in removing my doubt and unbelief from my mind.

But without faith it is impossible to please him: for he that cometh to God must believe that he is, and that he is a rewarder of them that diligently seek him (Hebrews 11:6).

Treatment in Progress

~Oh, what a beautiful morning, and I am so thankful to be alive. Today is my birthday, June 21, 2012. I woke this morning and received a pile of birthday cards mailed to me in one large envelope from my sister. She collected cards from church members, family, and friends and mailed them to me. A little later, I heard someone knock at the door, and there were flowers from my mom and dad and my brother and his wife; what a surprise! It is hard to believe that I am forty-six today. Of all places to spend your birthday — in a cancer center dedicated to natural healing through nutrition and non-conventional treatments.~

I had always considered myself to be "cold-natured." When it was summer and everyone was sleeping with just a sheet or a light blanket, I would be covered up with two or three blankets. I did not like cold weather, and when everyone was sweating beside me doing the same work, I would not even break a sweat. I never realized that my body should be getting rid of toxins by sweating. The oncologist told me that my whole endocrine system had shut down and was not releasing toxins.

When I arrived at the clinic, I was put in a sauna. At first, I sat and didn't break a sweat, and my husband came and laid hands on me and commanded my body to release sweat. Then I began to sweat in less and less time. What started soon would be more sweating than I had done in years. Soon I felt like every sweat gland in my body had opened up, and sweat was pouring off of me.

I had always tried to eat healthy, but now the meals are cooked in the kitchen of the clinic, and ***organic*** is the word and the law. The things added to our food in this society meaning to preserve the food are all considered bad by the clinic; whether it is meat, eggs, and even our bread, it is all loaded with preservatives and growth hormones which affect our bodies in a negative sense. I learned so much about natural, organic food preparation. I was there to get well, and so I listened and learned.

The detox foot baths stunned my eyes as black and rust colors formed in the water. Was this actually coming from my feet and my body? At first, I could smell a smell that I knew I had smelled before. I struggled to remember when and where I had smelled that smell, and then I remembered: When I had been a county coroner and had pronounced people dead who had died of cancer, there was a smell of their body that I now smelled. I told Dr. June that I could smell the smell of cancer in the toxic foot bath water, and she said that she had never had any one of her patients who could smell it. She said that she could smell it because she knew what it was but was surprised that I could smell it, too.

Over time, the foot bath water became clearer and clearer; however, if I had gone through tests with injections of radioactive material, then the toxic foot bath would contain dark, toxin-filled water.

~I have begun to sweat and exercise regularly for the first time in approximately thirty years. We have clearly seen God's hand at work. I went back to the doctor for a checkup, and he was so excited! He said, "God is still doing miracles! The tumors have all disappeared!" He told me that we might be looking at total remission already! I am doing very well and feeling stronger than I have in many years. This has been a time of standing on the promises of God's Word like never before, choosing to meditate upon the Word, day and night. I hate cancer, and God hates cancer. Jesus paid the price for our healing, and He rose from the dead, so that we will rise too. God is so good, and we are so thankful for all He has done. He has given us authority to operate here on earth, and it is so important that we walk in everything He has provided.~

While I was resting at the clinic, I told my husband I felt within me that something had clicked or turned the corner of recovery. This was exactly twenty-one days after Jesus had appeared to me, and I heard the word, "sweat." This is like the word Daniel received by an angel after he had prayed, and the angel said that he had been withstood for twenty-one days, the same time that Daniel had prayed:

Then said he unto me, Fear not, Daniel: for from the first day that thou didst set thine heart to understand, and to chasten thyself before thy God, thy words were heard, and I am come for thy words. 13. But the prince of the kingdom of Persia withstood me one and twenty days: but, lo, Michael, one of the chief princes, came to help me; and I remained there with the kings of Persia (Daniel 10:12-13).

However, my blood work came back on July 6, 2012, and my tumor markers were up, not down. I only told my husband. I had to fight a battle in my mind all day. I know that God is bigger than any report. Whenever I have done all to stand, I must stand, having my loins girded about with truth.

Wherefore take unto you the whole armour of God, that ye may be able to withstand in the evil day, and having done all, to stand. 14. Stand therefore, having your loins girt about with truth, and having on the breastplate of righteousness (Ephesians 6:13-14);

~I think that I snapped another tumor today, around my left hip; I was exercising, and now, I can feel my heart beating in my left hip, and I really hurt. I am staying focused on what Jesus has already done for me.~

We Were on Our Own.

~Today is July 3, 2012. We arrived back home three days ago. After a few nights of sleeping in our own bed, it was time to do all the things that had been done for us at the clinic, but this time without their nurses and dietitians. I wasn't worried. My daughter had been at the clinic learning how to start the IV's, and I was very confident that I could follow the food preparation, but little did I know what we would face.~

My daughter was nineteen and studying to be a veterinarian, but putting an IV in my arm with little veins would prove to be no small task. A part of my therapy was to begin the day with a nutritional IV with supplements to keep my body built up. This had been going on for two months at the clinic. My daughter was sure of herself, and she had watched and inserted the IV at the clinic with no problem.

Once, twice, three times – then six – and we could not hit the vein. My arm throbbed with pain, and my daughter and I were nervous wrecks. What had seemed so simple in a clinic, with nurses supervising, suddenly became impossible. We gave it up on day one after about ten tries; I felt like a pin cushion.

The next day, we would do no better, and by the third day,we were nearing mental collapse, as well as physical. We tried watching internet videos to see what we were missing and called different people to see if we could find a nurse to help us. It was so simple and easy at the clinic. Why had it become so difficult?

I called Evelyn, one of the ladies in our church. She worked at the hospital and told us that our problem was her specialty, for she had worked at the lab at the hospital for a while and could help us.

She came every day for a week, starting my IV and teaching my daughter how to do so. She taught Shanee how to feel for the vein and how to insert the needle properly. She brought some new needles and had Shanee practice on her arm. When Evelyn showed her that she could insert the IV anywhere in my arms, legs, or hands, Shanee became a natural, and we had no more trouble. What a relief for both of us!

If I had not had family and friends and a church to help, it would have been too much to purchase the equipment needed for my therapy; yet, it quickly came together. After an intense week of my husband's work, it was set up just like in the clinic.

I settled down into a daily routine to which I had become accustomed. Dr. June had told me that I must stay on my regimen and my therapy and stay on my diet until I went for my next full-body scan at the end of ninety days. I didn't go off my diet, and I stayed with the schedule.

Dr. June sent me extra IVs and my vitamins by Fed Ex whenever I needed them. The cost for my IVs was $150 each day for 5 days a week, a total of $750 a week. My vitamins cost about $1,000-1,500 per month. While I was at the clinic, the cost was about $350 per day, not including the cost of my vitamins.

The Spirit Came upon Me.

Many who grew up in the church may not feel it was all that eventful, but for me, one event would change my life. I had followed Jesus from the age of three and had made a public profession of faith in his salvation. Yes, I had believed; Yes, I was saved; but, I had heard about the baptism in the Holy Spirit with speaking in other tongues. Was it real? Could I receive it?

And when the day of Pentecost was fully come, they were all with one accord in one place.2. And suddenly there came a sound from heaven as of a rushing mighty wind, and it filled all the house where they were sitting. 3. And there appeared unto them cloven tongues like as of fire, and it sat upon each of them. 4. And they were all filled with the Holy Ghost, and began to speak with other tongues, as the Spirit gave them utterance (Acts 2:1-4).

One day, a Methodist minister stopped at Eastern Heights Baptist Church, in Cleburne, Texas, where my father pastored. He had written a book on Methodists receiving the baptism in the Holy Spirit and wanted to preach at our church if my father allowed it. "Yes," was the answer, and my dad asked him to preach that night, a Wednesday. It had begun to snow, and my father wasn't sure how many people would make it. The answer was not many; however, our family of six (my three siblings, myself and my parents) and six others came.

The preacher spoke very softly, and once the message was complete, he turned to the congregation and announced that he would lay his hands on anyone who wanted to receive the baptism in the Holy Spirit, and they would receive and speak in tongues. My oldest brother, my sister, and I went up front, hardly understanding, yet hopeful, to receive something from God.

This Methodist preacher was no fire-and-brimstone preacher; yet, he spoke with the confidence of someone who knew what he was doing. As I stood in front of him, I bowed my head and looked at his white patent leather shoes; then all of the sudden, my sister and I received the baptism in the Holy Spirit, and we began to speak in other tongues. Others received as well. The meeting was extended, and my oldest brother received the baptism in the Holy Spirit a night or two later. The meeting was all over in four services, but the church would never be the same. Later, that church would become one of the largest Spirit-filled churches in the city.

Now added to my study of the Scriptures and all I had seen in my parents was this spiritual awakening inside of me. What was this? I prayed daily in this new avenue of prayer, never understanding what had happened yet feeling exuberance as I prayed in these tongues of fire. The Holy Spirit had sat upon me as he had done in Acts 2:1-4.

But this is that which was spoken by the prophet Joel; 17. And it shall come to pass in the last days, saith God, I will pour out of my Spirit upon all flesh: and your sons and your daughters shall prophesy, and your young men shall see visions, and your old men shall dream dreams: 18. And on my servants and on my handmaidens I will pour out in those days of my Spirit; and they shall prophesy: (Acts 2:16-18)

Little by little, I would grow in faith. Over the next years and into adulthood, I would grow in what Jesus had talked about in the book of John:

Jesus saith unto her, Woman, believe me, the hour cometh, when ye shall neither in this mountain, nor yet at Jerusalem, worship the Father. 22. Ye worship ye know not what: we know what we worship: for salvation is of the Jews. 23. But the hour cometh, and now is, when the true worshippers shall worship the Father in spirit and in truth: for the Father seeketh such to worship him. 24. God is a Spirit: and they that worship him must worship him in spirit and in truth (John 4:21-24).

Now at forty-five, I was, according to the doctors, dying of a disease that I had often prayed against in others. Would all my life and upbringing be enough to carry me through this trial by another kind of fire?

I had seen others go through this disease that now consumed my body, and my experience was not at all encouraging, but I had to make a decision to not do things based upon my experiences with cancer but upon the solid truth of the word of God. I had seen many who knew what I knew about the things of God, and they died. I truly believed that God would deliver me, yet my soul (my mind and emotions) struggled at times, and I had to continue to renew my mind with the scriptures. I knew that the God I worshiped was real, and His word was true. I was calling upon Him, and I knew He would answer me. I would walk in everything I knew and see Jesus, my healer, deliver me.

I Learned to Pray in the Spirit.

I had seen my parents pray and had learned much in seeking after God. There were times that my Dad had gone into a time of intense praying in tongues. Groanings and utterances had come upon one or both of my parents as they had prayed for someone in the night:

Likewise the Spirit also helpeth our infirmities: for we know not what we should pray for as we ought: but the Spirit itself maketh intercession for us with groanings which cannot be uttered. 27. And he that searcheth the hearts knoweth what is the mind of the Spirit, because he maketh intercession for the saints according to the will of God (Rom.8:26-27).

Was there really any power in this spiritual exercise of intense praying in the Holy Ghost in tongues or in groanings that the Scriptures say is the Holy Ghost praying the will of God? There were no classes to learn how to pray in this manner. It would be strictly a Holy Ghost-taught experience based on the scriptures in Romans. It happened to me on many occasions over the years.

I had been in severe pain for days, ever since I had the second bone-strengthening infusion which was July 6, 2012. I had cried from pain more than I had ever cried in my life. I had never experienced pain like this. I was in so much pain that I was shaking very badly. I went to the bathroom and tried to use the bathroom but was shaking and hurting so bad I could not; my body was not working right. I came out of the bathroom, and Mark asked me how I was feeling. I was shaking and hurting so much that I could not talk. I went out to swim or at least get in the water to see if it would relieve some pressure because I knew that getting in water helps with the pain of childbirth. This was much worse than any labor pains that I had ever experienced in the birth of three children! Now, looking back, I really believed this to be a reaction to the bone-strengthening product the doctor prescribed and believe it to this day.

The first time I had the bone infusion, I had fever and flu symptoms, but this time the second, which was also the last, was horrible! I felt like my whole bottom swelled so much I could hardly use the bathroom and then only with excruciating pain. I have never hurt so much! This was even worse than childbirth and having an episiotomy on top of that; there was no comparison! This was a very difficult time for me. I passed out from the pain. I felt the tumors in my body growing, and I was having so much more pain. I continued to cast down my thoughts and imaginations. I knew I must stay in agreement with God's word. God's word is true: "Jesus Christ the same yesterday, today, and forever" (Hebrews 13:8).

For the weapons of our warfare are not carnal, but mighty through God to the pulling down of strong holds; 5. Casting down imaginations, and every high thing that exalteth itself against the knowledge of God, and bringing into captivity every thought to the obedience of Christ; (II Corinthians 10:4-5)

On July 9, 2012, I heard the words, "Discontinue use." I knew that this was referring to the Zometa that the doctor has given me by infusion. I prayed that God would show my oncologist and give him direction for my care. The next morning, I received a phone call from the doctor's office and the nurse said, "Shirley, the doctor said that he thinks you should ***discontinue use*** of the Zometa and just see how you do." I cried and thanked God for his Holy Spirit leading me and guiding me and sending me to a doctor that could hear the voice of God too. I was so relieved.

We left the next morning to drive to the Dallas area for the tests. I was in so much pain all I could do was cry. I was breathing like I did giving birth to my children to help reduce the pain and stay focused, trying to get some relief. I could not speak; I could only pray in tongues and cry. I couldn't sit down or lean back in the car. Mark had placed pillows all around me to help me get comfortable, but the pillows did not help. I could not even stand to put my seatbelt on because the pain was so great that I wanted to just go back home! I continued to meditate on God's word. I could not read; it was too hard.

Mark turned on a Kenneth E. Hagin, Sr., sermon on the testimony of his healing. He shared of how he was meditating on a Scripture portion from the gospel of Mark:

And Jesus answering saith unto them, Have faith in God. 23. For verily I say unto you, That whosoever shall say unto this mountain, Be thou removed, and be thou cast into the sea; and shall not doubt in his heart, but shall believe that those things which he saith shall come to pass; he shall have whatsoever he saith. 24. Therefore I say unto you, What things soever ye desire, when ye pray, believe that ye receive them, and ye shall have them (Mark 11:22-24).

He said that as he was meditating on these verses he saw and received his healing by faith. Within minutes, he was being healed and came out of a bed of paralysis and was healed of a deformed heart and incurable blood disease — not in days or weeks, but minutes!

I began to groan in the spirit as I heard his testimony; no words, I just groaned and groaned in prayer so hard in my innermost being, and I received my healing by faith. Within minutes, all the pain was gone! It was as if it just melted away, from my head throughout my body. The Spirit of God had quickened my mortal body. There is so much power in the testimony of what Jesus did.

And I fell at his feet to worship him. And he said unto me, See thou do it not: I am thy fellowservant, and of thy brethren that have the testimony of Jesus: worship God: ***for the testimony of Jesus is the spirit of prophecy*** *(Revelation 19:10 emphasis mine).*

I once heard a message taught by Bill Johnson at Bethel in Redding, California, and he shared on the power of the testimony. He stated,

"Every testimony contains all the elements to reproduce another testimony. I had always noticed when I would minister and share a testimony that the Holy Spirit would hover over the testimony, and it would move the hearers into faith-filled encounters with God.

Confess your faults one to another, and pray one for another, that ye may be healed. The effectual fervent prayer of a righteous man availeth much (James 5:16).

Lessons and information were either gleaned or reiterated during this battle:

Remember in the Bible where Elijah had gone to pray:

So Ahab went up to eat and to drink. And Elijah went up to the top of Carmel; and he cast himself down upon the earth, and put his face between his knees, 43. And said to his servant, Go up now, look toward the sea. And he went up, and looked, and said, There is nothing. And he said, Go again seven times. 44. And it came to pass at the seventh time, that he said, Behold, there ariseth a little cloud out of the sea, like a man's hand. And he said, Go up, say unto Ahab, Prepare thy chariot, and get thee down, that the rain stop thee not. 45. And it came to pass in the mean while, that the heaven was black with clouds and wind, and there was a great rain. And Ahab rode, and went to Jezreel (I Kings 18:42).

Elijah prayed until the answer came. Faith moves God.

Now faith is the substance of things hoped for, the evidence of things not seen (Hebrews 11:1).

Faith is the substance (there has to be substance), something tangible, an act of some kind. Move towards God, act on his word. Whatever you do, do it in faith.

*But without faith it is impossible to please him: for he that cometh to God **must believe that he is**, and that he is a rewarder of them that diligently seek him (Hebrews 11:6 emphasis mine).*

Jesus prayed in groanings:

When Jesus therefore saw her weeping, and the Jews also weeping which came with her, he groaned in the spirit, and was troubled, (John 11:33)

Two times over Jesus would pray in groanings:

Jesus therefore again groaning in himself cometh to the grave. It was a cave, and a stone lay upon it (John 11:38).

I could not help but see this as a foretaste of:

Likewise the Spirit also helpeth our infirmities: for we know not what we should pray for as we ought: but the Spirit itself maketh intercession for us with groanings which cannot be uttered (Romans 8:26).

I believe that groanings in the Spirit can even raise the dead. Many times we don't know how to pray, and we can allow the Holy Spirit to pray through us and change the circumstances around us. The Holy Spirit quickens and makes alive every cell of our mortal being.

But if the Spirit of him that raised up Jesus from the dead dwell in you, he that raised up Christ from the dead shall also quicken your mortal bodies by his Spirit that dwelleth in you Romans 8:11).

When we receive Jesus as our Lord and Savior, we are changed and transformed into his image, his likeness and his ways.

Know ye not that ye are the temple of the God, and (that) the Spirit of God dwelleth in you? (I Corinthians 3:16)

What? Know ye not that your body is the temple of the Holy Ghost(which is) in you, which ye have of God, and ye are not your own? (I Corinthians 6:19)

The Ninety Days Pass

The daily routine of my therapy was practically an all-day affair, starting with juicing every morning just before or with my breakfast. Later, I would have an IV in my arm while I sat with my feet in the foot bath that always seemed to take longer than I wanted. This was usually followed by time on the RIFE machine. Then, it was usually time for lunch, followed by exercise and sitting in the sun for thirty minutes. After exercising and the sun, I would sit in the sauna for 35-45 minutes, after which I had to shower and lie down to rest for a while. By the time it was over and dinner was cooked, the day was gone. Day after day staying on the same routine; how I wanted to get up and just go to work -- but I wasn't about to jump ship!

Sunday was the bright spot since I was allowed to skip the IV and the exercise. Church was my oasis of joy. Sometimes I testified of what was happening to me, and sometimes I was too tired to say much.

Every Sunday, I saw hope. The ninety days were passing quickly, and soon I would go back for another full-body scan that would tell me how far I had progressed.

Finally, it was time to return. Thoughts were trying to torment me, "What will I do if the cancer has spread and not gone away?" I would think of this sometimes just for an instant, and then I would rebuke the enemy. Sometimes I felt like the man with the lunatic child:

And straightway the father of the child cried out, and said with tears, Lord, I believe; help thou mine unbelief (Mark 9:24).

Three Months' Checkup

~Tuesday, August 21, 2012, we are driving back to Dallas for another round of tests for my three-month checkup. My husband has been fasting every Tuesday since my diagnosis, but today was different. He was told by the Holy Spirit not to fast this Tuesday; it would be a time of celebration.~

We had woken up early to get ready for my PET scan at 9:30. I was very dizzy, and Mark went to get me a glass of water. I drank some of it and could taste the chemicals in it. I have only been drinking bottled water or reverse osmosis water. I began to throw up all the water and was still very dizzy. I did not know what it was from. I thought it could just be because of nerves or another attack of the enemy.

We were staying at the La Quinta Inn next to Baylor Hospital in Plano, Texas. I got up to go to the bathroom and couldn't even stand. Shanee got up to help me to the bathroom. I was sick in my stomach and very nauseated. Shanee helped me get my sweat suit on. I could not have any metal on me for the PET scan. I could not even walk by myself without falling. This was so crazy, but I knew to keep praying in the Holy Ghost, for I knew:

(For the weapons of our warfare are not carnal, but mighty through God to the pulling down of strong holds;) (II Corinthians 10:4)

Mark helped me across the road to the hospital, brought me to the waiting room and sat me down. I was so dizzy that Mark had to check me in. We sat in the waiting room for some while, waiting for my name to be called. Finally, I heard, "Shirley," and my heart rate felt as if it began to speed up. I had to walk down a hall, then turn, then down another hall. I was already dizzy and this was making it even worse. I continued to pray in the Holy Ghost. They took me into the same room I was in for my first PET scan. The same man that did my injection the first time was now giving me another. I was injected with a sugar-based radioactive material that would go and attach to cancer in my body.

I continued to pray in tongues, building myself up in faith:

But ye, beloved, building up yourselves on your most holy faith, praying in the Holy Ghost, (Jude 1:20)

I received a text message from Mark who was out in the waiting room since no one could be around me after the injection because I was radioactive. The text said, "I love you, forever." I began to cry and was so thankful for such a godly man who has stood with me in faith, boldly declaring the Word of God over me.

Then the man came into my room after an hour and said, "It is time." He took me across the hallway to the PET scan machine and had to help me because it felt like the whole room was spinning. I finally laid down in the machine and heard that still small voice, "I'm confirming my word with signs following." I laid still for the next hour with my arms up over my head, flat on my back, but in great peace, thanking God for confirming His Word. I got up after the tests were over, and I felt so much better; the dizziness was almost completely gone. I am so thankful for the Word of God that was hid in my heart even from the time I was a little girl. Many times you don't realize the importance when you are young, but later in life, you see how important your foundation really is.

My Foundation

I was raised in a family who loved God. We were always at church on Sunday morning, Sunday night, and Wednesday night, and if there was a revival going on, we never missed a night. We were always so busy at church that we did not have time to get into trouble. I grew up with a great reverence and fear of God. I saw a Holy God and I so wanted to stay in His presence. The Lord Jesus was the center of everything in our lives, and the Scriptures received special attention. When I was a little girl, I remember my daddy seating us on the bed and reading the Bible to us. Later, we would read it ourselves together, every night for seven years. I know the Scripture my father and mother followed:

Train up a child in the way he should go: and when he is old, he will not depart from it (Proverbs 22:6).

My whole life had been intertwined with prayer, the church, and the Bible. To me it had been an exciting life, growing up with the reality of Christ and the Holy Spirit. It had all seemed so natural. After that first seven years, I didn't need any help to continue reading the Bible; it was just natural.

The baptism in the Holy Spirit with a flowing of tongues was just as natural:

And suddenly there came a sound from heaven as of a rushing mighty wind, and it filled all the house where they were sitting. 3. And there appeared unto them cloven tongues like as of fire, and it sat upon each of them. 4. And they were all filled with the Holy Ghost, and began to speak with other tongues, as the Spirit gave them utterance (Acts 2:2-4).

I grew up never wondering about whether God was real. I knew my salvation experience had happened when I was very young. I cannot remember a time that I did not know God or believe in Him. He was my Lord Jesus Christ. My father was a teacher of the word, and I had listened intently in church as he had explained truths that sparked my mind and moved my spirit. It seemed the Spirit of God had opened my heart to see and believe in Him as a child, and I rejoiced in that knowledge.

And that from a child thou hast known the holy scriptures, which are able to make thee wise unto salvation through faith which is in Christ Jesus (2 Timothy 3:15).

My grandmother, Virgie Whitehead, raised her children to serve God. Her daughter, my mother, had conveyed it to me in a soft spirit. All of my mother's family had been raised in church and had either married preachers, become pastors, or worked in church; indeed, I had a foundation to stand upon. My parents had pastored churches all my life. I had so many memories of praying for the sick, and the testimonies were thrilling.

I will never forget the night we went to a revival center called Souls Harbor in Dallas, Texas, for a seminar with evangelist W.V. Grant, Sr.. I was about three years old, and I saw the crippled get up and walk, the blind see, and tumors disappear. One woman had a large tumor on her forehead that had some fluid oozing out, and as Brother Grant stretched out his hand to touch her, the tumor disappeared before my eyes. I had crawled under the seats in front of me to get a better view, and I was forever changed as the glory of God filled the place. Many repented and called upon Jesus to be their Lord and Savior.

Is any sick among you? let him call for the elders of the church; and let them pray over him, anointing him with oil in the name of the Lord: 15. And the prayer of faith shall save the sick, and the Lord shall raise him up; and if he have committed sins, they shall be forgiven him (James 5:14-15).

Jesus was the healer; even in Sunday School, I learned of Jesus opening the blind eyes, healing the woman with an issue of blood, and restoring the crippled. The word of God had come alive in my life, and the words that Jesus spoke had meaning and power:

It is the spirit that quickeneth; the flesh profiteth nothing: the words that I speak unto you, they are spirit, and they are life (John 6:63).

Jesus had even raised the dead:

Jesus saith unto her, Said I not unto thee, that, if thou wouldest believe, thou shouldest see the glory of God? 41. Then they took away the stone from the place where the dead was laid. And Jesus lifted up his eyes, and said, Father, I thank thee that thou hast heard me. 42. And I knew that thou hearest me always: but because of the people which stand by I said it, that they may believe that thou hast sent me. 43. And when he thus had spoken, he cried with a loud voice, Lazarus, come forth. 44. And he that was dead came forth, bound hand and foot with graveclothes: and his face was bound about with a napkin. Jesus saith unto them, Loose him, and let him go (John 11:40-44).

I had been raised to believe that God could and would heal the sick and even raise the dead. Often, I had overheard my parents praying for someone to be healed, and sometimes they would cast out demons; this was our normal life.

I had always loved a challenge, and when my dad asked me to go on an upcoming mission trip, I willingly agreed. But, little did I know how much it would affect my life. We traveled extensively in the Yucatan Peninsula and had to use machetes to cut through the jungle to make our way back into some areas. Many churches were planted during this time, and a genuine work had been birthed that would soon reach the nation. We had been witnessing to a village and bringing the gospel, and one day we were back in the village of Senor, and a man came to get Brother Bob Smithee our missionary to come to this other village. So, a group was gathered together and went to the village. The mother of the leader of the village had died days before, and they remembered that the missionary had told them of a God that raised the dead, and now it was time to put God on display. Well, Bob was anything but a normal missionary. He just knew God had called him to bring the good news to these people, and was ready to walk out the scriptures. So, he went to the lady that had been dead for days and prayed for her, and God raised her from the dead. Because of this event, the entire village came to know Jesus as Lord and Savior, and to this day, they serve Him. Needless to say, this really changed me and all the others in this ministry during this time. I spent enough time in Mexico to learn a language that would help me tremendously over the years to come. I was able to stand upon the word of God for myself, and I began to walk in the power that Jesus gave us in Luke 10:19. I saw first hand that demons had to go in the name of Jesus. As the Holy Spirit began to reveal Jesus to me in a new and fresh way, this revealed revelation began to change every aspect of my life.

After being in the Yucatan in Quintana Roo, Mexico, on this extended mission trip, I was returning home shortly after my sixteenth birthday. I'll never forget arriving back at Oklahoma City Airport, where my parents were waiting for me. I had been gone for a while, and the church had been in a time of fasting and prayer for forty days. My parents had both lost a lot of weight, and I almost didn't recognize them. Not only had they lost weight, but I, too, had lost weight after being on a diet of fresh fruits and vegetables in the jungle of Quintana Roo, Mexico, and working in a village of Senor with our missionaries, Bob and Rose Smithee and their family. I am eternally grateful for the opportunity that was given to me and so thankful that Bob and Rose Smithee heeded the call and obeyed. The work in Mexico continues to this day under the direction of Bob's son, Rory Smithee, and his wife, Flora Smithee (a native Maya Indian from the village of Senor).

I was a very busy teenager. I loved to learn and never wanted to be left out of anything. At school, I was president of the Student Council and president of the Spanish Club, and involved in almost everything. I worked at a restaurant at night, taught aerobics to the ladies at church, worked in children's church, was in the youth band, and kept up a 4.0 grade-point average, all at the same time.

I would hurry home and get ready to go to another meeting, knowing I needed to get home to finish studying. I had to get up early to go to work at my second job as a home health-care provider. I went before school and gave a shot of insulin to a diabetic. "If it was easy, God would have called someone else," was my father's favorite saying whenever I complained.

My parents had been in ministry all my life. We were raised in church, and our lives were totally committed to serving. It wasn't always easy being the "preacher's kid," but I knew how blessed I was to be in a household of faith. I always felt like the only important thing I could ever do was to serve God with all that I had. I had the greatest examples around me, my parents, who poured the Word of God into me from the time I was very young.

What precious times I remember when I was young as I crawled up on my parent's bed as we had "Bible Time." My parents shared with us as the Holy Spirit revealed Christ Jesus as Lord and Savior through the Scriptures. I gave my life to Jesus on that king-size bed, was later baptized in water when I was six years old, and received the baptism in the Holy Spirit and my prayer language when I was eight. My family wasn't like most other families, I later found out.

There was a time that I thought all fathers sat on the floor cross-legged, praying in the Holy Spirit, reading the Word, and receiving direction and insight for the day and things to come. I found out later just how unusually special our family truly was.

I grew up in a home where we waited on God to hear His voice. We were taught to be sensitive to the leading of the Holy Spirit and allow Him to pray through us. My dad showed us the importance of hearing the voice of the Spirit of God. I knew that Jesus said that He was seeking those who would worship Him in spirit and in truth. I knew one word from God would change everything, and we were to be willing and obedient.

My mother had grown up in a household of faith, and we have many relatives in the ministry on my mom's side. My father's family was a different story. He was raised in a household where his dad made moonshine in a still, drank whiskey, and lived an ungodly life. My dad gave his life to the Lord at nineteen and was called to preach shortly after being saved. He led his entire family to the Lord, and they were all filled with the Holy Ghost. Even his grandpa had a mighty revelation of God and was saved and baptized in water when he was seventy-two.

My husband, Mark Williams, and I married when he was 28 years old, and I was 18 years old in 1984. We met at a small church in Lookeba, Oklahoma. When Mark was 25 years old, he heard a message on being specific when you pray. At this time in his life, he was looking for a wife since he had already graduated from college and was working as a geologist. He set aside some weeks to assimilate a list of what he wanted in a wife. He divided this list into three categories: spiritual, mental, and physical – and in that order. His desires for a wife were that she must have been a Christian for many years, from a household of faith under parents who were still married. This, he felt, would bring stability in one's walk with the Lord. Another spiritual attribute he had listed was being spirit-filled, which promotes a deeper walk with God.

The mental elements he listed included being emotionally sound, of a good attitude and wise beyond her years. He listed, too, that she must be smart (I did graduate valedictorian of my class from Tecumseh High School in Oklahoma in 1984.).

This list physically went like this: 5'6" to 5'7" tall, long blonde hair that could be worn straight or curly, blue eyes, like to dress up and wear heels, be physically healthy, and weigh 120-140 pounds.

My husband had seen God answer so many prayers before and knew that if God placed these things in his heart then God was also able to bring this woman into his life. So he prayed to God for his wife and mentioned these things to the Lord to fulfill.

After we were married, I was unpacking things to get settled in the home we were staying in, and I found a list in his handwriting simply titled: "What I want in a wife." I began to cry as I read the list, realizing that he wrote all these things two years before we even met; I was so touched. He came home from work shortly thereafter, and seeing that I had been crying, asked me if everything was okay. I showed him the paper that I found and explained that my tears were more about realizing how much he really did seek me and how God brought us together.

My foundation was solid, and when I married, I was anxious to tell the world about Jesus, Lord of All, Savior, Healer, and Redeemer. My husband was committed, and what I lacked, he provided. He had lived in Tulsa, Oklahoma, and sat under the teachings of Kenneth E. Hagin, Sr., one of the founders of what is called the "Faith Movement", along with Kenneth Copeland

Over the years of our marriage, Mark was always like an oak tree, firmly planted in the word of God. His great faith surely helped me to recover from cancer. On the day that we stood in front of the church that we pastor, he proclaimed to the church that we would not walk through the Valley of the Shadow of Death; we would run through it! Daily, Mark stood with me in faith – every step of the way.

This journey would have been very difficult without the help of my family. Mark and all the kids changed with me. They ate what I ate, juiced with me daily and everyone stepped up to exercise with me. I never felt alone in the journey, and for that, I am exceedingly grateful. Now, the whole family has become very attentive to what we all put into our bodies. We are all healthier, and we have all come to a place of deeper accountability in spirit, soul and body.

Bone Density Scan

Thursday, November 29, 2012, we left Marathon and headed to Dallas to stay at Dr. June's clinic. I was scheduled to undergo a bone density scan the next morning. I was so tired of tests and more tests and always feeling like a pin cushion, but I was also at the same time very excited every time I heard the next good report.

We got up early the next morning, November 30, 2012, and went to Garland for the bone density scan at 8:30 a.m.. It was by far the easiest test up to this time. After leaving this test site, we went to see Dr. Olivares at Texas Oncology. I always arrive a little earlier than my appointment to get my blood drawn, so the doctor can look at my results. They have a lab right there in the facility. Dr. Olivares is always so kind and considerate and always makes me feel the deep compassion coming from him, and today was no different. They called my name, and Mark and I went back to the room awaiting the doctor's arrival. I was really anticipating good news, but the enemy is always trying to mess with your mind, trying to put thoughts of doubt and unbelief in your head; but, you have to continue to remind yourself of what God says about you. In walks Dr. Olivares and he pulls my records up on the computer screen in the room. He began to tell me that all my blood work looked excellent and normal. He then looked over the results from the bone density scan, and he was excited! He went on to explain that all of my bone density results were excellent, and I had the bones of a sixteen-year-old! I am so thankful to the God that never leaves me and never forsakes me. He is with me always, even through the storms of life and makes a way of escape.

My Diet

The food preparation was, at first, not that difficult. My uncle and aunt gave me a nice juicer to begin my juicing, so the first thing I needed was supplied. Every day I juiced four carrots, a cucumber, and a small beet, all organic. It became very expensive when I had to buy organic vegetables. My parents, sister, and many friends brought me organic vegetables from their summer gardens. We had a small garden, and one day as I walked out into the garden, I said, "Lord, I need a cucumber today, so I can juice. I am out of them." I went over to the cucumber plants which I had been watching closely awaiting a sign of up-and-coming cucumbers. There was one cucumber on the vines, just one, but that was what I had asked for that day. Then, I began to thank the Lord for the cucumber, and I knew I was not to limit God. I began to thank Him of an abundance of cucumbers. I watered the garden and the greenhouse and prayed over the plants, then I started back to the house.

When I was getting close to the house, I heard a diesel engine. I thought it was my husband, and I wondered why he was back from work so soon. I went to the front of the house to check on him, but it wasn't him. It was one of my friends from a local ranch. I went to greet her, and she explained that she had just picked her garden and wanted to know if I could use some fresh vegetables, as she had an overabundance. I was so excited! She had bags and bags of cucumbers!! I had more cucumbers than I could have imagined! Oh, the God we serve is more than enough. The abundance kept coming: squash, peppers, cucumbers, tomatoes, and much more. When I told some of the church people, I had so much food arriving that we had squash for breakfast, lunch, and dinner.

Then the same lady who brought me the cucumbers had moved to another ranch house, and she had planted a large garden at the first house, close to town. This lady told me to go and pick whatever I needed and could use from her garden because it was all organic! What a great blessing for me since we had very little availability of organic food. I knew it was a gift from God!

We had tomatoes, cucumbers, peppers, squash, lettuce and spinach – more than we could absorb. We juiced and canned until we could do no more. My mother bought me a canner and some canning jars, and soon, I was given more and more jars and food to can.

My daughter, Shanee, helped me in the kitchen, gave me IVs, helped me pick gardens, canned, and coached my exercise program and still studied and attended classes at the university. All of this hands-on experience and visiting Dr. June's clinic (where I had stayed for the last sixty days) caused her to become very knowledgeable in organic cooking.

I had always tried to eat healthy, but this was a new dimension in food preparation – cooking everything from scratch and learning what all I could and could not have. For example, I could only have grass-fed beef and free-range chickens fed with grains without growth hormones. Indeed, it was a whole new world that I was growing more knowledgeable of every day. Now that I was feeling a little better every day, I pressed on.

We also needed some beef and meat that I could eat. Dr. June had told me I could eat sardines and wild-caught salmon, some organic beef, wild-caught fish, buffalo, goat, and deer or elk meat. The purchase price of organic beef was costly if one could find it. One of the men in our church told us that he had grass-fed beef which he normally processed in the winter. But if Mark, the twins, Vaughn, and Shanee would help him, he would slaughter and process one for us. They all went the next week and worked for two days helping slaughter, process, and wrap all the meat. We were able to fill our freezer with organic beef for much less than the cost of meat from the natural food stores.

A man in our church owns a food distribution business (mainly supplying restaurants) and found organic food items for me. I could buy a case of organic items, and it would reduce the price of the items to the cost of regular, non-organic items from the grocery store. He also found organic chicken at less per pound than what was available in larger cities (plus it was delivered at our store!).

I learned so much about preparing food that I could eat. My daughter and other women in the church all looked for recipes that were simple that I could make without any of the "banned foods" in them. There was so much that I could not have and a lot of new products that I had never used.

Nothing gives one a greater motive to live than being given a death sentence.

The Exercise Continues.

I had allowed my body to go down over the last year since I began to feel the pain in my breast, and I really had gone down in physical strength.

The doctor told me to swim and exercise moderately, but after a few months I knew it was time to begin to rebuild my muscles. Even a few minutes of exercise overwhelmed my weakened body in the beginning, and I would lie exhausted on the floor. Within a few days, I knew I could steadily increase the amount of exercise by only a few minutes each day.

I had once been an aerobics instructor and could exercise seemingly without an end of my strength. Now, I began to exercise five minutes, then pushed to ten minutes, then onto fifteen minutes, twenty, and soon up to thirty minutes. It all came slowly, but I was coming back.

I would swim since it was summer, and I would feel better after swimming.

After a few months, I started the "Insanity" exercise program. My daughter coached and encouraged me to go on. At first, I could only do it for a little while, but I would do all I could, then rest awhile, and do a little more. Over time, I got better and better until I was able to exercise along with my daughter. I could feel life pulsating through me. I was alive again! I continued the "Insanity" exercise program for a period of about five months straight, and afterwards have continued to exercise and do different programs to maintain my strength and stamina. I am so blessed that I have been given another opportunity to live again, and live more abundantly!

*Beloved, I wish above all things that thou mayest prosper and be in **health**, even as thy soul prospereth (3 John 1:2 emphasis mine).*

Dream of Cancer in Reverse

One week before I was scheduled to return to Garland to see the doctor for another bone scan, I had a dream.

I dreamed that Mark and I were driving on a highway. Mark was behind the wheel, then I saw him burst out laughing, and he put the gas pedal to the floor. I looked, and the vehicle was in reverse. We began to go faster and faster on the highway, and my heart was racing.

When I woke up, I heard the Spirit speak to me, "This is the rate of which I have reversed the cancer." I cried and cried, thanking God for reversing it all. I also repented for not taking better care of myself.

Thou hast turned for me my mourning into dancing: thou hast put off my sackcloth, and girded me with gladness; (Psalms 30:11)

A merry heart doeth good like a medicine: but a broken spirit drieth the bones (Proverbs 17:22).

I was overcome with excitement the day that I read this scripture:

What do ye imagine against the LORD? he will make an utter end: affliction shall not rise up the second time (Nahum 1:9).

I knew the God I had served continually was not only able to deliver me as He did, but it would not come back on me a second time. Jehovah Rapha -- the Lord that heals me and keeps me well.

I saw that I touched God on covenant. The scriptures tell us that we are under a new and better covenant and that I had entered into a covenant relationship with Jesus through believing upon Him, making Him my Lord and Savior, Healer, and Deliverer. I was no longer dependent upon the Sovereignty of God. I had a covenant with Him, and He would not break His covenant. The Holy Spirit revealed this to me, and I could walk in this revelation. I saw so many of God's people dying for lack of revealed knowledge.

My people are destroyed for lack of knowledge: because thou hast rejected knowledge, I will also reject thee, that thou shalt be no priest to me: seeing thou hast forgotten the law of thy God, I will also forget thy children (Hosea 4:6).

War with My Mind

~February 26, 2013, we are driving to Dallas today. Last week, I had two fever blisters come out on my lip, and I knew it was from stress. It has been several months since my last appointment, and I am scheduled to have a full-body bone scan tomorrow. We are driving to Dallas and will stay at Dr. June's clinic tonight, so we can head to the oncologist's office in the morning.~

~February 27, 2013, We arrived at Dr. June's clinic last night and took a shower and went right to bed. I am on my way to the Nuclear Medicine Department of Texas Oncology, today.~

Mark drove me to the areas of Baylor Medical, Texas Oncology, in Garland, Texas, with Dr. Olivares. My appointment was at 10 a.m.. As we arrived, I could feel my heart racing. Even as I walked up to the registration desk, it was still pounding. Thoughts were racing through my head, "What if the cancer is still in your bones? The pain that you have felt in your hips -- what if the cancer has spread?"

Oh, the torment of the mind and thoughts that were going on in my head! It was hard to imagine how difficult these last weeks have been. I have had to continually pray in the Holy Ghost. I have had to stand and keep standing on God's word, casting down imaginations:

(For the weapons of our warfare are not carnal, but mighty through God to the pulling down of strong holds;) 5. Casting down imaginations, and every high thing that exalteth itself against the knowledge of God, and bringing into captivity every thought to the obedience of Christ; (II Corinthians 10:4-5)

I kept reminding myself because the Holy Ghost would remind me and say, "Shirley, it is not your flesh and blood that you are wrestling with; it is the principalities, powers, and rulers of darkness of this world; against spiritual wickedness in high places that you are warring." (Ephesians 6:12 paraphrased).

So I would stop and take the authority given to me:

Behold, I give unto you power to tread on serpents and scorpions, and over all the power of the enemy: and nothing shall by any means hurt you. (Luke 10:19)

I would say, "I have power and authority over all demonic forces that have come to hurt me, and in the name of Jesus, I bind you, spirit of infirmity, cancer, and pain, in the name of Jesus. I command you to Go! Go! Go! I don't want you, and you have no right in me. I am free! I am healed! Jesus bore all my pain, all my sickness, and by His stripes, I am healed! With my heart, I believe, and with my mouth I confess that Jesus is Lord over every area of my life, spirit, soul and body. The same spirit that raised Christ Jesus from the dead dwells in me, quickening, making alive my mortal body. To every cell I speak LIFE in the name of Jesus."

Then I felt the Holy Spirit impress on me, "Shirley, don't be conformed to this world's way of doing things, but be transformed by the renewing of your mind. You are proving my will."

I beseech you therefore, brethren, by the mercies of God, that ye present your bodies a living sacrifice, holy, acceptable unto God, which is your reasonable service. 2. And be not conformed to this world: but be ye transformed by the renewing of your mind, that ye may prove what is that good, and acceptable, and perfect, will of God (Romans 12:1-2).

Out of MY belly flows rivers of living water, and Life and Death are in the power of MY tongue.

Death and life are in the power of the tongue: and they that love it shall eat the fruit thereof. (Proverbs 18:21)

This has been a new revelation to me: that if any man can control his tongue, he can control his entire body. I continued to be reminded by the Holy Spirit to not be overcome with evil, but to overcome evil with good. We overcome by the blood of the Lamb and the word of our testimony.

That if thou shalt confess with thy mouth the Lord Jesus, and shalt believe in thine heart that God hath raised him from the dead, thou shalt be saved. 10. For with the heart man believeth unto righteousness; and with the mouth confession is made unto salvation. (Romans 10:9-10)

This scripture in Romans became more real to me than ever before. The same way that He gave me citizenship in the kingdom of God by confessing Jesus with my mouth and believing in my heart that God raised Jesus from the dead is the way to total salvation, salvation for the spirit, soul, and body! The Greek word, "Sozo" comprises salvation for the whole man. Jesus did a complete work, and as I read Ephesians Ch.1, I saw a new revelation. I had been taught before, but now knew by revelation that because of what Jesus has done on the cross for me — he had brought all things under His feet but also under my feet. This is all possible because I am seated with Christ Jesus in heavenly places.

Then I heard the attendant call: "Shirley Williams," and a volunteer took me and my husband to the next waiting room in the Nuclear Medicine Department. Another volunteer in that area greeted us. I waited for a short period, and then a woman named Rose came and asked me to follow her. I followed her down a hallway to a room. I asked if my husband could come with me, and she said, "No." This lady named Rose then proceeded to tell me how she was going to inject radioactive material into my vein that would go straight to my bones, and the areas that had cancer would have an uptake, and then the doctors would be able to see it on the bone scan. After she injected me, she told me I could go and eat and come back at 1 p.m. for the scan.

Earlier this morning, I woke and began praying for a woman who had been diagnosed with breast cancer, but I had not met her in person. I had only spoken with her over the phone. Well, while I was praying for her by name, the phone rang, and it was her. I had heard about her through Betty, a lady in our church. Betty had encouraged her to call me. This woman had already been through surgery, a double mastectomy, and was undergoing chemotherapy. I knew I was to meet her and pray over her. I knew I had to bind a spirit of fear, rebuke it, and command it to go in the name of Jesus.

We decided to meet for lunch at Chipotle's at 11 a.m. after my injection. We arrived early at 10:45 and waited in the car. It was a very cold day, and I could feel the humidity in the air. I was talking on my cell phone with Shanee when the woman I was to meet tapped on my window. She was about my size, with blonde hair, and she was so precious, but she was so afraid! I could see it all over her. I knew that look, and I remembered it all too well!

As I sat across the table from her, I could not contain myself as I began to share with her that with God, nothing would be impossible! **His word is True.** Let every man be a liar, but God's word is TRUE! That faith is the substance — and there is substance – in faith. Faith is an act and faith acts! Even if you don't see it, ACT! All the promises of God are "Yes" and "Amen!"

I reached across the table and took her hands and began to speak out loud! Yes! Right in the middle of Chipotle's with people all around. I bound a spirit of fear and commanded it to GO! Get out of her in the name of Jesus! Tears ran down her face as we came into agreement with God. Sitting right in front of me was a woman that had been diagnosed after me. Her hair was thinning from chemotherapy, both breasts had been removed, and once again, I knew except for God, I would have been there, too. She kept commenting on my hair. She said, "My hair was like yours. I chopped it all off, and my hair is shedding." I cried out to God for her. Oh, the compassion that God has for us!

For God so loved the world, that he gave his only begotten Son, that whosoever believeth in him should not perish, but have everlasting life (John 3:16).

Wow! Oh, how He loves us! Well, it was already time to head back to the hospital. After the injection, I had to stand spiritually; we don't walk by feelings, but by faith. The fear that had gripped me was hard to fathom! The word says that we are to pray for others so that we ourselves may be healed.

Confess your faults one to another, and pray one for another, that ye may be healed. The effectual fervent prayer of a righteous man availeth much (James 5:16).

As I reached across the table to pray one last time for her, I took authority over fear, not only for her, but to remind myself that God had not given us a spirit of fear but of power and love and a sound mind. If God didn't give us a spirit of fear, then who do we think it came from? It is a spirit of fear, not just fear, but a spirit of fear. So, since we have been given authority over these spirits, we must act upon that authority. I commanded the demon spirit of fear to GO! I knew I couldn't allow it to come on me. I had to stand on God's word!

I felt a gripping pain hit me in my chest, my back, and in my hips. I immediately began to speak over my body, commanding pain to cease, pain to go in the name of Jesus! Then the pain left!

We arrived back at the hospital again, this time for my scan. As I walked in, I had faith in my heart. I began to thank God for making me completely whole, completely well, and totally restored! At the same time, there was doubt trying to flood my mind. You can have faith in your heart and doubt in your head, but press on; it is with the heart that man believes unto right standing with God, and it is with the mouth that confession is made unto our salvation (sozo), our healing.

I was taken back to the same area where I received the injection earlier, but now taken into a room. I crawled up on the machine. I lay down, and I was so cold. The man performing the scan wrapped a warm blanket over my body. I had to have my arms straight down to my sides, and the man told me to be very still.

He began to explain the scan procedure to me as he taped my feet together with masking tape. The machine began to move from my head to my toes. I was so glad when the machine had passed below the tips of my fingers, and I heard him say, "You can put your hands across your body now, but keep the rest of your body still." My fingers were tingling from keeping my arms to my side without moving. I was glad to now be able to move my arms.

The man told me about gamma rays, and I thought about the Incredible Hulk. Finally, the test was over, and the man helped me get up. I was still shaking a little inside as I stepped on the stool then down to the floor. The man reached over and helped me put my jacket back on, and then he handed me a card that showed that I was radioactive, just in case someone needed to know. I thought it was a little hilarious when I looked at the card the nuclear physicist gave me because it said that the card would expire on 2/30/2013. I guess he didn't catch the mistake, for February only has 28 days! Well, I thought it was funny after such a stressful time in that machine!

~Tomorrow is my mother's birthday; she told me that she only wanted a good report for her birthday. We obtain a good report by faith!

For by it the elders obtained a good report (Hebrews 11:2).~

Confirming My Healing

~February 28, 2013 -- as I woke up this morning, I heard in my spirit these words, "the miracle of the loaves and fishes."~

I began to think about this after I was totally awake. I knew that the miracle took place in the hands of the disciples as Jesus placed the bread in their hands; as they broke it, it multiplied. I knew Jesus had given me authority, and He had put it into my hands.

Many times we cry out to God for God to do something, but He has already delegated authority to us. He is wondering why we are not using the authority He has given us. We expect the Head (Christ Jesus) to do something that the Body (we the believers) should do. No wonder the Word says, "My people perish from lack of knowledge."

After waking, Mark and I got ready to go to the doctor's office for the results of my scan. I heard someone in the kitchen, and Mark went to see who was there; it was Dr. June. She had arrived early to see us. It was so good to see her again. We spoke for a few minutes and then left for the doctor's appointment. Mark pulled into the parking lot of the hospital where we had gone yesterday, and I reminded him we were going to see the oncologist today. While he was driving out of the parking lot to go down the street a short distance to the next office, I saw Rose, the woman who did my injection the day before.

I was very moved in my spirit to pray for Rose. I had already spoken to Rose on several occasions. She was the one who had performed the first nuclear bone scan last year. I knew she was a Christian because I asked her when we first met. As Mark drove to the doctor's office, I continued to pray for Rose. We walked into the building, went to the elevator like we always did, and went to the second floor. It seemed very different this time. I kept praying in tongues. I knew I was about to get the results from the nuclear bone scan that had been performed the day before. All types of thoughts were racing through my head: thoughts of doubt and unbelief, "what ifs," and so much more. But, I knew that I had to keep casting these thoughts down in the name of Jesus.

(For the weapons of our warfare are not carnal, but mighty through God to the pulling down of strong holds;) 5. Casting down imaginations, and every high thing that exalteth itself against the knowledge of God, and bringing into captivity every thought to the obedience of Christ; (II Corinthians 10:4-5)

I kept speaking the Word over myself; I kept saying, "I am healed. Jesus took all my pain, all my sickness, and by His stripes, I am healed; with the heart, man believes unto righteousness, and with the mouth, confession is made to salvation." "Whosoever shall call on the name of the Lord shall be saved. Out of my belly shall flow rivers of living water." I said, "God, don't forget our covenant relationship. You said all the promises of God in Christ Jesus are 'Yes' and 'Amen' to me." "I receive it now." I was speaking quietly, reminding myself of everything I had seen God do in my life. I was reminded of David as he went to slay Goliath. He remembered all that God had done for him.

I walked into the doctor's office, signed in and sat down to wait for them to call my name and for my blood to be drawn, so the doctor could check on my levels before I went in to see him.

As I sat down, I kept praying in tongues, and I knew I was praying for Rose. Then a woman walked into the office, signed in, and came and sat down beside me. I turned to introduce myself to her. She responded and said, "My name is Rose. I have cancer and don't have long to live." I knew she was the Rose I had been praying for. I began to tell her about Jesus, and I took my husband's Bible and began to show her the scriptures. I shared with her:

But what saith it? The word is nigh thee, even in thy mouth, and in thy heart:

that is, the word of faith, which we preach; 9. That if thou shalt confess with thy mouth the Lord Jesus, and shalt believe in thine heart that God hath raised him from the dead, thou shalt be saved. 10. For with the heart man believeth unto righteousness; and with the mouth confession is made unto salvation (Romans 10:8-10).

As I read to her, the nurse called my name, and Rose said, "Wait. I want to make sure I am going up and not down." She said, "I have never heard what you have shared with me today. I said, "Don't worry, Rose. My husband is here, and he will pray with you and make sure you receive Jesus as Lord." I told her, "It is okay; he is a pastor." She said, "Well, good, then it will be done right." I said, "Yes, it will."

Then I went in for my blood work. I went from the lab to the doctor's office and waited in the room for Mark to meet up with me. While I was waiting for Mark, I found some information on bone cancer. I began to read and began thanking God for making a way for me to be healed. I began to say, "Thank you Jesus for making me whole."

When Mark met up with me, he said, "Rose received Jesus!" Shortly after, the Doctor came into the room, and we shared with him about Rose receiving Jesus in the waiting room. He was so thankful.

Then he pulled up my information on the computer and looked at my bone scan. After he pulled up my first bone scan and compared it to the new bone scan, he stopped and scooted his chair back and looked at me and said, "Your bones were clear!" He went on to say that he had seen two medically documented healing miracles, and I was one of them. He said, "All that jumping and pounding you did exercising caused your bones to rebuild. Your bones look like the bones of a teenager!" He went on to tell me the following, as he leaned forward in his chair toward me, "In all the years that I have been an oncologist, I have had many people tell me that they were healed, but I have only seen two medically documented healing miracles, and you are one of them."

I could hardly contain myself, I was so excited! Every emotion known to man began to flood out of me! I could not contain my feelings. I cried; I screamed with thanksgiving, laughed, jumped, twirled around in circles, and jumped again! Even as I am writing this the emotions are uncontrollable. I am so thankful that Jesus came to me and made a way of deliverance for me, a way of escape. Oh, the joy that floods my soul that I serve a resurrected Lord! He knows where we are and what we need. We must learn to hear the voice of God and walk in His way, for the words that He speaks to me are spirit, and they are life.

We bubbled with praise to God. I thought about all my struggle of the last many months while my life hung in the balance, and now I was on the other side! I called my mother and told her the good news, and she was elated! We all thanked God for providing healing for us all. I am so thankful that Jesus took from us all of our sickness and all of our diseases, and by the stripes he bore upon His back, I am healed. Praise God! Thank you, Jesus!

Brought Test Results to the Nutritionist

After we left Dr. Olivares' office, we took the test results to Dr. June at her clinic in Richardson, Texas. When she read the test results, she went throughout the clinic telling other patients over and over, **"Stage 4 Cancer – GONE!"**

I remember the others: God has given me so much, but I could not get out of my mind the faces of all those other women I had seen waiting for test results, radiation, or chemotherapy in hospitals, waiting rooms, and doctors offices. In my mind's eyes, I can still picture them fearful, hopeless, despairing, and in pain! What I saw in their faces makes me want to go and tell each of them what happened to me. I am cancer free! Praise God!

I knew I would have to write a book and tell everyone there is hope in Christ Jesus. There is hope in the Word of God; they have to hear His voice and follow Him. I want to encourage them that they could and would need to learn how to hear a Rhema word, to hear "*This sickness is not unto death.*"

And hear Him who said:

My sheep hear my voice, and I know them, and they follow me: (John 10:27)

And other sheep I have, which are not of this fold: them also I must bring, and they shall hear my voice; and there shall be one fold, and one shepherd (John 10:16).

They would need to hear when He said:

And Peter answered him and said, Lord, if it be thou, bid me come unto thee on the water.29. And he said, Come. And when Peter was come down out of the ship, he walked on the water, to go to Jesus (Matthew 14:28-29).

I knew I should write everything: all my fears, my weakness, my faith, and my failures, desires, and pain. I would tell it so that any other woman who will ever face this, has faced it, or is facing it can have hope.

When the doctors had told me that I had only ninety days to live, I went to see my mother and father. His words were classic: "Well, Baby," he said, "if you get up close to death, spit in its face because no one can have faith when they are full of the fear of death," for the scriptures say:

Forasmuch then as the children are partakers of flesh and blood, he also himself likewise took part of the same; that through death he might destroy him that had the power of death, that is, the devil; 15. And deliver them who through fear of death were all their lifetime subject to bondage (Hebrews 2:14-15).

There is no fear in love; but perfect love casteth out fear: because fear hath torment. He that feareth is not made perfect in love (I John 4:18).

I determined that I would cast out all fear and replace it with faith in God and His word. Now, I have passed through the fear of death, and I have seen Him who is stronger than death.

O death, where is thy sting? O grave, where is thy victory? (I Corinthians 15:55)

I have come to a personal conviction that all sickness and disease is of the devil and that we have been authorized, delegated, and commissioned to walk in the authority that Jesus gave us in Luke 10:19 as believers and to cast out unclean spirits of all kinds so that those who are bound and sick can be free and well.

I had come to the place where it no longer matters:

For whether we live, we live unto the Lord; and whether we die, we die unto the Lord: whether we live therefore, or die, we are the Lord's (Romans 14:8).

Yet, here I am alive and well and thankful for both. Now, I must tell all those others who I passed by on the road to recovery about Him who is Jehovah Rapha, the Lord our Healer. He has raised me up to live again.

And Jesus went about all the cities and villages, teaching in their synagogues, and preaching the gospel of the kingdom, and healing every sickness and every disease among the people (Matthew 9:35).

Crossing Over

~I woke up this morning with a song, "Come morning, you'll find me touring that city where the Son of God is the light". My mother sang this song at my grandfather's funeral, and I knew that my Uncle Farris also must be close to death. We went to church this morning, September 1, 2013, and after service, we went to the local health food grocery store to pick up a few items. Before I went into the store, I called my parents who had left Midland to head to Cleburne to be close to my uncle and aunt. Uncle Farris had been asking for my dad to come. My mother and Uncle Farris are siblings. Our families grew up together as my Uncle Farris and Aunt Susan had been in ministry with my parents when I was young. They ran a mission in Cleburne, Texas, together for years. The church that my Uncle Farris pastored, Eastern Heights Church, was the church I grew up in, and my dad was the the senior pastor there years earlier. I was born and raised in Cleburne, Texas.~

Over most of my life, I had noticed that the Holy Spirit would show me things to come many times, events that would take place that day so I would be ready. I would dream and wake up with a word or just a knowing. I knew that if I wanted to see my uncle alive, I would need to head that direction. During my conversation with my parents, they told me that Uncle Farris had been asking for my dad to help him cross over. Uncle Farris had been in and out of consciousness for a few days. It was very hard on all of us since our families have always been very close. My cousins and my siblings all grew up together, and we were more like brothers and sisters than cousins, spending a lot of time at each others' houses; my dad and Uncle Farris were also much alike, both preachers that gave their lives entirely to preaching the gospel. They took the part where it says, "Go into all the world and preach the gospel" as a personal mandate, and God was depending upon them to make sure it was done. They both made all the kids work, and they always had another project going on, and both were builders of the Kingdom of God. My dad performed our marriage ceremony, and my Uncle Farris walked me down the aisle. Oh, I always loved my daddy, but I also loved my Uncle Farris. He had a more gentle nature, and I always wanted to marry someone like my daddy and Uncle Farris. When I met Mark, he reminded me so much of both of them, such a hunger in him to go after God, and I told him that. I just knew Mark was the one for me.

Farris had been diagnosed with multiple myeloma years prior and had a very difficult walk through the years. The family prayed and prayed for him, and he stood on the Word of God.

I will never forget the day we went to visit my relatives and went to Eastern Heights Church on that Sunday morning. Uncle Farris had fallen outside on his hip and went to the doctor and had received an awful prognosis. They had given him about nine months to live. He continued to speak the Word over his body and soon was able to get up and walk again. It was a very difficult time on the entire family. He would sit in a recliner in the church and get up and sit on a stool and would preach with such powerful anointing. This particular morning, he was preaching on Psalms 91 -- a sermon I will never forget; he repeatedly would say, "Surely, He shall deliver me." Then, he would share some more and again would say, "Surely, He shall deliver me." Soon, the entire church would come into agreement with him. Soon, he would be back in full force, walking and preaching all over the stage.

He would pray before he ate and say, "He blesses my bread and my water." He always encouraged me to never focus on what the doctor's had said but to only meditate on God's Word.

I called on February 28, 2013, and told Uncle Farris that all the bone cancer in my body was gone; it had all reversed. I had just left the doctor's office, and I was so excited I couldn't wait to call my Uncle Farris. He was so happy for me and told me, "Whatever you do, don't get off track." Those words still resonate in me today. I knew that the Holy Spirit was speaking through Farris to warn me to continue abstaining from sugar, eating well, including organic foods when possible, exercising and doing what Jesus told me to do, " Sweat". Also, I knew that he meant to continue to fortify my body with minerals and vitamins, but above all, never lose faith and trust in our Lord Jesus Christ who directed me to total health. My Uncle Farris had been through so many treatments for so many years, both conventional and non-conventional, and he shared with me how difficult it had been, and he was tired. His physical body had been so broken down due to many of the treatments that his body did not respond well to.

The next morning, September 2, 2013, early in the morning, Farris took his last breath and crossed over into glory -- no more sorrows, no more pain, no more sickness, no more disease. I don't understand why he died, and I can't answer all the questions, but I knew I must keep my eyes on Jesus. Oh, it was so hard, and oh, the thoughts that tried to torment me, but I had to make myself focus on the Word of God, constantly reminding myself to keep my eyes on Jesus.

This boulder called cancer looked so big for so long it was like Goliath, but we continued to push up against this boulder, and now, it is in danger of moving, and it is being totally removed from my path. For as we have pushed, our strength has increased, and the Holy Spirit brought revelation, and now, cancer will have to bow its' knee to the name of Jesus.

I cried out over and over to God, and I was reminded of when Moses was crying out to God. With the Egyptian army on one side and the Red Sea on the other, Moses had just prophesied, and then he begins to cry out to God. Then God said, "Moses, why are you crying out to me? What do you have in your hand?" (Exodus 14:15,16 paraphrased) Well, he had the rod which would represent the authority that we have as a believer, and it was time to use it. He was told to stretch forth his hand, and the waters parted, and they crossed over on dry ground, and then as the army tried to cross over after them, they were all swept away in the water.

Farris told me, "Don't be afraid. Cancer is nothing to be afraid of." He told me that he was so thankful that I got on a fast track and avoided many missteps that he had taken through his journey, and he was so grateful that I had not gone through traditional conventional treatments. He so encouraged me through a phone call or text to check on me. He always had an encouraging word.

I had to make some decisions to keep myself from discouragement because it will lead to the **sin of unbelief**. That which is without faith is sin. He that cometh to God must believe that He is, and that He is a rewarder of them that diligently seek Him.

When we begin to walk in the authority that has been given to us as a believer, our lives change forever. When we know who we are and whose we are, we walk into the revelation of the righteousness of God in Christ Jesus. We then pass it on to generations to come. A righteous man leaves an inheritance for his children's children.

Tragedy has been very foreign to our family; it is not that we haven't had to deal with some very rough times and set backs, but my uncle's departure has really been rough on all of us. Don't ever fill your heart or eyes with the crisis. The same faith that has brought us to victory is the same faith that will help us deal with our loss. I could not allow myself to focus on any weakness, only the Word of God. I had to see how strong Christ is in me. I know that I know that I know that it is Christ in me, the hope that God will be glorified here on this earth. The only thing that I know to be true is the Word. This is the foundation on which I stand.

In Hebrews chapter eleven, the faith chapter, God shut the mouths of the lions; mighty men and women moved God by their faith, and God was shutting the mouths of the lions that came at me. So many people came to me trying to console me, but I couldn't allow myself to go there. We all have losses from time to time and trials and disappointments, but NEVER focus on the storm, always keep your eyes on Jesus! I know that we are right there with those in the faith chapter. So many people never believe for a miracle; they just try to keep us from getting our hopes up. Stay away from those people; fire those doctors! Jesus paid the price, took our sickness and our pain, and by his stripes, we are healed! I challenge you to believe again! Keep your eyes on Jesus!

I hate cancer! I am praying for everyone with cancer, making a demand on what belongs to us through what Jesus has provided. I'm walking in the victory, knowing that Satan is defeated. A natural hate won't do a thing, but a supernatural hate will empower you. Learn to love what Jesus loves, and hate what Jesus hates.

I have seen the dead raised, tumors disappear before my eyes, crippled get up and walk, blind eyes open, deaf ears open, and missing body parts grow back. I have seen the Glory of God manifested, and I am so thankful that He has continued to show up and manifest His glory. Whatever city or town we go into, we are told to heal the sick there. Where? Whatever city or town you go into. You got it right, wherever you are. Go into all the world and preach the gospel. Where is your world? The place where you live. That is your world. Quit waiting for another mission trip or some revival. Revival begins when the people go out and bring the lost in. Stop waiting for your pastor or an evangelist. Get up and do something now. Change your world, so they can be transformed to become like Christ Jesus, the anointed One.

This Book Only Promotes Christ Jesus.

This book is not promoting a nutritional approach to sickness – neither vitamins, diet, nor exercise. I am only saying that is the way He led me.

I am not saying that you should disregard the advice of your doctor if he or she tells you that surgery is for you; I am saying that it was not the door for me. I am saying that each of us must learn to be led by the Holy Spirit and the Word of God. I realize that this is not the lifestyle of many, yet, it is the only one I can recommend. To find a cure of cancer that was throughout my body in the equipment, vitamins, nutritional IVs, or diet is to miss the power and direction of God that flowed through our lives during this time.

Jesus answered and said unto them, Ye do err, not knowing the scriptures, nor the power of God (Matthew 22:29).

Below is the concept as seen in the scriptures concerning the brazen serpent that Moses had built according to the direction and the commandment of God. This brazen serpent is like seeing all the things God used in my deliverance from cancer and seeing them as the answer. We must look through them to see Jesus, the Word of God, and the Holy Spirit directing us to the end result:

The Brazen Serpent

And they journeyed from Mount Hor by the way of the Red sea, to compass the land of Edom: and the soul of the people was much discouraged because of the way. 5. And the people spake against God, and against Moses, Wherefore have ye brought us up out of Egypt to die in the wilderness? for there is no bread, neither is there any water; and our soul loatheth this light bread. 6. And the LORD sent fiery serpents among the people, and they bit the people; and much people of Israel died. 7. Therefore the people came to Moses, and said, We have sinned, for we have spoken against the LORD, and against thee; pray unto the LORD, that he take away the serpents from us. And Moses prayed for the people. 8. And the LORD said unto Moses, Make thee a fiery serpent, and set it upon a pole: and it shall come to pass, that every one that is bitten, when he looketh upon it, shall live.9. And Moses made a serpent of brass, and put it upon a pole, and it came to pass, that if a serpent had bitten any man, when he beheld the serpent of brass, he lived (Numbers 21:4-9).

1. The people had been bitten by deadly snakes.
2. They would die shortly if God did not intervene.
3. God instructed Moses to make a brass serpent and put it on a pole.
4. Whoever looked on the serpent would live.

Neither let us tempt Christ, as some of them also tempted, and were destroyed of serpents. 10: Neither murmur ye, as some of them also murmured, and were destroyed of the destroyer. (I Corinthians 10:9-11)

1. Our worship and our sight must be on Him alone;
2. We must see Him as the full payment for our sin;
3. He, alone, destroyed the power of sin and death.

He removed the high places, and brake the images, and cut down the groves, and brake in pieces the brazen serpent that Moses had made: for unto those days the children of Israel did burn incense to it: and he called it Nehushtan (II Kings 18:4).

Hezekiah broke in pieces the brass serpent:

1. Hezekiah saw that Israel had made the brass serpent into a substitute for God.
2. They worshiped the object and not the God that gave them the object.

3. The brass serpent was a type of Christ, but it was not the Christ.

And as Moses lifted up the serpent in the wilderness, even so must the Son of man be lifted up (John 3:14).

1. Jesus, in this scripture, showed that He was the fulfillment of the brazen serpent.
2. Jesus, on the cross crucified, was payment for the serpent's bite (sin and death).

Ye worship ye know not what: we know what we worship: for salvation is of the Jews (John 4:22).

Do you know what you worship?

1. Whenever God's people worship anything other than Christ and Him crucified, they miss the truth of God.
2. The brass serpent was only the object that pointed them to Christ Jesus, Himself.
3. We must look to Jesus, the one — and only one — who is our Salvation, Healer, and Deliverer!

The Overall Direction

There are many things included in this book:

1. The great emphasis on the Word of God being my life
2. Prayer in many forms:
    A. Calling out to God in simplicity
    B. Praying in other tongues
    C. Praying in groanings and utterances
    D. Praying the scriptures
    E. Confessing the Word in Prayer
3. Casting out devils
4. Speaking to a disease as though it was a spirit

All of these may be new to the reader but not to the one who walked through this valley. I would point the reader to a slow reading of Matthew, Mark, Luke, and John for a greater understanding. This book follows the footsteps of Jesus through the Gospels, believing that every word in them is true.

What Do I Mean by a Rhema Word?

When Jesus spoke to his disciples, he said:

It is the spirit that quickeneth; the flesh profiteth nothing: the words that I speak unto you, they are spirit, and they are life (John 6:63).

You must learn to hear His voice.

The first step is to become immersed in the Word of God.

Learn to wait before God in prayer.

Those who seek Him will find Him.

No one can do it for you.

My Final Word

Since my diagnosis and freedom from sickness and disease, I have had many people come to me and ask me to pray for them, and I do. Many have asked me to hear God for them and then tell them what God said. I prayed many times, feeling like there was something I needed to see. I was reminded of the disciples who walked with Jesus and were part of His ministry while they were with Him; they saw so many mighty miracles. They were like a small vehicle caught in the draft of an eighteen-wheeler truck or like someone riding in the wake of a large ship. As soon as Jesus was taken from the disciples, Peter denied Christ. They had been moving in the flow of the spirit that Jesus had with the Father. Jesus told the disciples and others in Acts 1:8 that they would be endued with power from on high after the Holy Ghost came upon them. Jesus instructed them to not leave until they received the baptism of fire and became totally immersed in the Holy Spirit. They needed their own personal encounter with God. No one could do this for them; they each needed to know God for themselves. They waited for the Upper Room experience:

And when the day of Pentecost was fully come, they were all with one accord in one place. 2. And suddenly there came a sound from heaven as of a rushing mighty wind, and it filled all the house where they were sitting. 3. And there appeared unto them cloven tongues like as of fire, and it sat upon each of them. 4. And they were all filled with the Holy Ghost, and began to speak with other tongues, as the Spirit gave them utterance (Acts 2:1-4).

Going to church does not give you the key to eternal life. You must believe upon Jesus and have a personal encounter with the Triune Godhead. The Holy Spirit will draw you to the Father and reveal Jesus as Lord. When temptations come, when difficulties and storms of life bombard us, we know whom it is we serve, who it is that we can depend on – the One who knows us and has the right answer and will show the way of escape to each of us.

I encourage you to make Jesus your Lord today. Call upon Him, and He will answer you and show you great and mighty things that you don't know:

But what saith it? The word is nigh thee, even in thy mouth, and in thy heart: that is, the word of faith, which we preach; 9. That if thou shalt confess with thy mouth the Lord Jesus, and shalt believe in thine heart that God hath raised him from the dead, thou shalt be saved. 10. For with the heart man believeth unto righteousness; and with the mouth confession is made unto salvation (Romans 10:8-10).

Ask him to fill you with the Holy Spirit, and you will receive a prayer language from heaven. When you pray, the Spirit of God will pray through you. Go ahead; ask Him to manifest himself to you. He will; expect it to come, for it is with the heart that we believe, and it is with the mouth, we confess that Jesus is Lord.

You cannot just think it; you must say it. You must know Him and the power of His resurrection. You must understand that you must first believe that God is (that He exists) and that He is a rewarder of those who diligently seek him:

But without faith it is impossible to please him: for he that cometh to God must believe that he is, and that he is a rewarder of them that diligently seek him (Hebrews 11:6).

May 19th, 2013, over a year from the time I was told that I had a short time to live, I was sitting in the sun thanking our Lord for healing and saving me from my destructions. This was a special day because I am with my family all gathered around, enjoying this evening and watching my second daughter, Shanee, being married to a special man, Josiah Obbink. Many people came to congratulate me as the mother of the bride, as it was meant to be. Jesus said, "I have come to give you life and life more abundantly." I cherish these words with real meaning now, especially on this day. I praise Him with all my heart.

Now, my family continues to grow. We gained a son-in-law and our oldest daughter, Shatiel, and her husband, Adam, just had another child, our first grandson. I am so proud of them. Now, I am a grandmother for a second time. My husband and I are enjoying being grandparents. We take many pictures with joy in our hearts and on our faces. It is especially great to see myself in some of these pictures. I am grateful to God for these exhilarating moments to live them in fullness, joy, and HEALTH!

Years later after being diagnosed with cancer, we continue to pastor where God has so graciously planted us in Alpine, Texas, and I am so honored to get to travel and share the testimony of Jesus in my life and His resurrection power. Many are receiving healing from all manner of sickness and all manner of diseases through teaching the body of Christ how to be led by the Spirit of God, hear His voice and walk it out in faith.

A Sudden Attack on Our Pastors (by Betty Jones, Intercessor and Deliverance Minister)

It was such a sudden attack! A surprise attack without any warning!

Immediately, a "chain reaction" of prayer began. People of faith were calling people of faith. The shield of faith was raised up to quench all the fiery darts of the enemy. We needed an absolute miracle! Besides my mom being raised from the dead, I knew I was about to be a witness to one of the most incredible documented miracles I had ever seen!

Our covenant rights of healing were being declared and stood upon. Cancer was being commanded to leave Shirley's body. We continued to do this until the total manifestation of her miracle was complete.

Wellness began to come. It was a process. Day by day...... we stood and continued releasing our faith ... the substance of things hoped for!

Shirley's dad said it was to be a 100-day battle. We were not begging or pleading but TAKING and STANDING on the covenant. We were COMMANDING cancer... "GO NOW! You must leave. You have no choice."

We spoke, "principalities and powers, rulers of darkness and spiritual wickedness in high places, you will turn Shirley Williams loose!" We bound the Spirit of premature death, destruction and torment. "Devil, you are defeated and a liar, and YOU WILL GO! NOW! Shirley will fulfill her destiny and call to the nations."

Epilogue: Integrative Medicine's Approach to Treating Cancer (by Dr. June Meymand)

Patients who receive a diagnosis of cancer are completely overwhelmed and full of fear, but I believe today, more than ever before, it can be the most amazing time to have cancer due to Integrative Medicine.

Oncologists are educated and trained to treat cancer with chemotherapy, radiation, and surgery. That is where their focus has been, and rightly so, because we as a society should understand that we need to have a TEAM of doctors working together in the best interest of the patient. This team should include an oncologist, a surgeon (if required), and last but not least, the patient. Yes, I said the PATIENT. A person needs to be responsible for their life, their health, their state of being, and therefore, must be a critical part of this team.

Each of these doctors will meet, test, diagnose, and make recommendations for treatment to the patient. The integrative medicine doctor with specialty in clinical nutrition for cancer patients is going to oversee the patient's entire body: biochemically, physiologically, nutritionally, and emotionally to keep this patient as healthy as possible while fighting cancer. To do this takes many years of experience working with all types of doctors and patients to give the patient the best possible chance to LIVE, not just exist during cancer treatment.

The black hole of cancer treatment today is clinical nutrition, specific to a cancer patient's biochemical needs. For years, patients have been told to try to eat well but eat whatever possible to avoid losing weight and wasting. Why? Because an estimated 40% of cancer patients die of STARVATION; however, the answer is not eating, "whatever." The answer is quite different for each patient and each patient's specific needs based upon several factors:

1. What kind of cancer was diagnosed?
2. What are the recommendations of their oncologist?
3. What is their medical history?
4. What has been their diet and exercise program for the last several years?
5. What kind of job do they do and many other factors.

Each member of the team has to work together in the best interest of the patient. There is no room for statements like, "Chemotherapy will kill you!" or "You might as well put a fig leaf on your head and dance in the light of a full moon as to see an integrative medical doctor."

Your team has to have doctors who know their respective degrees well and who respect other doctors who are well educated and experienced in their degrees. There is no doctor who knows it all in every specialized field. Your doctors are not GOD and should be relieved that another member of the team is there to watch over the patient's needs -- which bring me to faith. Eat, sleep, breathe, and know that you will get well. This is in GOD'S hands!

God bless you,

Dr. June Meymand, BS, DC, HME, FIAMA
Board Certified in Integrative Medicine,
Diplomate in Clinical Nutrition-Cancer

I, as the patient, Shirley Williams, never doubted that I had been led by the Spirit of God to go to Dr. June Meymand's Healing Arts Cancer & Wellness Center in Dallas, Texas. Dr. June's treatment of diet, exercise, vitamins, juicing, organic foods, and the use of various pieces of medical equipment would prove to be a deciding factor in my recovery.

My father, Cordell W. Mitchell along with my mother, Odena L. Mitchell, who contributed so much revelation of the Word of God into my life, wrote the following books:

SNAPSHOTS OF CHRIST in GENESIS
SNAPSHOTS OF CHRIST in EXODUS
SNAPSHOTS OF CHRIST in LEVITICUS
SNAPSHOTS OF CHRIST in DOCTRINE
SNAPSHOTS OF CHRIST in ORDINARY LIFE
SNAPSHOTS OF CHRIST in I KINGS
SNAPSHOTS OUT OF THE MOUTH OF CHRIST
"WHO DO MEN SAY THAT I AM?"
SNAPSHOTS OF CHRIST IN ISAIAH, VOLUME 1

Other suggested readings:

THE BELIEVER'S AUTHORITY (Kenneth E. Hagin)
CANCER FREE, ARE YOU SURE? (Jenny Hrbacek)
WHO SWITCHED OFF MY BRAIN? (Dr. Caroline Leaf)
EAT THIS AND LIVE (Dr. Don Colbert)

CPSIA information can be obtained
at www.ICGtesting.com
Printed in the USA
FSHW020105130120

9 781478 725404